Freedom's Ground

TEACHER'S EDITION

Unit 3   Riding High

Freedom's Ground

Bernard J. Weiss
Lyman C. Hunt

Educational Consultants
Eloise Eskridge / Janet Sprout / Millie Moore

Holt, Rinehart and Winston, Inc.
New York · Toronto · London · Sydney

TEACHER'S EDITION

Unit 3 Riding High

Bernard J. Weiss / Lyman C. Hunt / Maeve Finley / Barbara Horner / Sarah Throop

Acknowledgments

Grateful acknowledgment is hereby made to the following authors, publishers, agents, and individuals for their special permission to reprint copyrighted material.

Abingdon Press, for "One for the Univac" from *The Terrible Troubles of Rupert Piper*, by Ethelyn M. Parkinson. Story copyright © 1956 by Abingdon Press.

The Bobbs-Merrill Company, Inc., for "Robert H. Goddard: Father of the Space Age," adapted from *Robert Goddard: Pioneer Rocket Boy* by Clyde B. Moore, copyright © 1966 by The Bobbs-Merrill Company, Inc.

Dodd, Mead & Company, Inc., for "Computers in Our World," from *The New World of Computers* by Alfred Lewis, copyright © 1965 by Alfred Lewis. Reprinted and adapted by permission of Dodd, Mead & Company, Inc.

E. P. Dutton & Company, for "Earth, Moon and Sun," and "Blue" from *Poems of Earth and Space* by Claudia Lewis, copyright © 1967 by Claudia Lewis. Reprinted by permission of E. P. Dutton & Company, Inc.

Alfred A. Knopf, Inc., Murray Pollinger, agent, George Allen & Unwin Ltd., for "The Television Chocolate-Room," adapted from *Charlie and the Chocolate Factory* by Roald Dahl, copyright © 1964 by Roald Dahl.

Holt, Rinehart and Winston, Inc., for excerpt from *Language and Thinking in the Elementary School* by E. Brooks Smith, Kenneth S. Goodman, and Robert Meredith, copyright © 1970 by Holt, Rinehart and Winston, Inc. Used by permission.

McGraw-Hill Book Company, for "What Television Is," from *Television Works Like This,* by Jeanne and Robert Bendick, copyright © 1965 by McGraw-Hill, Inc.

May Swenson, for "The Cloud-Mobile," copyright © 1958. Reprinted by permission.

United Feature Syndicate, Inc., for "Peanuts," from *Peanuts` Revisited,* copyright © 1957 by United Feature Syndicate, Inc.

World Publishing Company, and Curtis Brown Ltd., for "By the Light of The Moon," from *Moon in Fact and Fancy,* by Alfred Slote. Text copyright © 1967 by Alfred Slote. Reprinted by permission of the World Publishing Company.

The authors gratefully acknowledge the valuable help of the following teachers and editors: Judith Adams, Sara Butte, Marguerite Fuller, J. Alice Hofler, Barbara Lyons, Blair McCracken, Carlene McNeil, Elizabeth Park, and Lome Piasetsky.

Developing Teaching Strategies

Stimulating a young person's love of good literature and developing his abilities to interpret and understand what he reads are the main goals of this series. The Teacher's Edition of *Freedom's Ground* is organized toward these ends; the teaching strategies and suggested lessons in it serve as models for developing appropriate skills. From the rich variety of material included—marginal notes, exercises, and commentary—*the teacher is urged to select what is appropriate for the interests and abilities of her pupils.*

Each of the six units, annotated pupil pages supplemented by teacher commentary, is bound separately for convenience and ease of handling. In addition, a separate introductory booklet contains a statement of the overall approach to the teaching of reading, and an extensive index to the skills developed.

THE UNIT INTRODUCTION

The Introduction to each unit provides a quick overview of the content of the unit. Next, The Enrichment Program describes the recordings, the sound filmstrips, and the Satellite Books prepared especially for the unit. This is followed by a Bibliography, a list of recommended books which may be drawn from the school library before beginning the unit and made available for the classroom reading table.

OVERVIEW OF THE TEACHING PLAN

Preceding each selection, the teacher is given a brief summary of the story, pertinent biographical data about the author, and a list of materials helpful in teaching the selection—filmstrips, recordings, Satellite Books, workbook pages, and Evaluation Masters. The section called Human Values offers some general but significant goals for possible development during the discussion of the story.

Under Objectives, specific skills are identified. While these skills, which may be taught and tested before the lesson is completed, form an instructional core for each lesson, they are not to be considered a limiting factor. Teacher judgment will dictate suitable strategy in line with her total instructional program.

THE TEACHING STRATEGIES

The segment of the lesson plan just described supplies a background for management which precedes engagement with the reading group. In Teaching Strategies, direct involvement with the group begins. The teacher-pupil elements of the plan are these:

Word Highlights. This section is designed to develop the vocabulary the pupils will encounter when reading the selection. The sets of exercises are also concerned with establishing basic lexical principles, the emphasis varying from selection to selection. Thus, an opportunity is provided to present examples of structural analysis, phonetic analysis, etymological principles, semantic variations, and rhetorical devices. This word study is extended and reinforced on subsequent pages by annotations alongside the text.

Introducing the Selection. Suggestions here are motivational and involve discussion, based upon pupil experience, to develop concepts intrinsic to an understanding of the story. Background information is given, and interests are stimulated before silent reading is assigned.

Guided Silent Reading. This section sets up specific purposes for reading. In most instances, these purposes are to be placed on the chalkboard before the group is assigned to read the selection silently.

Interpretation and Comprehension. After the selection has been read silently, the group assembles for discussion. The questions and activities accompanying each pupil page provide opportunities for oral reading, for language analysis, for critical reaction, and for fun and enjoyment. The questions recognizing individual needs are on several levels of difficulty. They should be used selectively.

The annotations in the upper margins of these pages are also designed for selective use. They provide many opportunities for literary comment and word analysis in terms of definition, structure, and function. The teacher may wish to interweave them in the discussion, or she may complete the discussion and then refer back to whatever annotations are appropriate for the group. They are not intended to be used as exercises for mastery, but as an additional commentary clarifying the text. The annotations also suggest correlation with all the language arts and help in fulfilling the stated objectives.

Reading and Language. This section of the lesson plan develops the objectives stated at the beginning of the lesson and represents a systematic approach to the study of language. Under Reading Skills, model exercises cover the areas of phonology, morphology, semantics, syntax, comprehension, and study skills. Under Literary Skills, additional opportunities are provided for critical thinking, literary analysis, and appreciation of the rhetorical devices used in the text.

Regrouping for Individual Needs. The regrouping exercises provide reteaching for pupils who need it, as well as extension activities for those ready for deeper exploration of selected skills. These exercises serve as models and should be used selectively to meet varying abilities. Evaluation Masters are available with the program and may be used before the reteaching activities to help determine individual needs.

Enrichment. The activities in this section suggest a wide variety of experiences, some for the superior pupils, some for the less gifted. They are humanistic in feeling and frequently relate the language arts to the fine arts, the social studies, and the sciences. This is yet another strategy for individualization in terms of abilities.

Unit Review. At the end of each unit under Summary Activities are suggestions for reviewing and discussing the theme of the unit and comparing the selections in terms of genre, story structure, and characters encountered. Review Exercises cover much of what was taught under Reading and Language in the unit, emphasizing reading skills, literary skills, and study skills. Also, there are some suggestions for creative activities.

The teaching strategies described here incorporate a total-language approach to reading, with many opportunities for reinforcement, individualization, and creativity. The plan provides a greater variety of material than the teacher can use with each group, but by doing so, the authors enable the teacher to meet a wide range of pupil needs.

Table of Contents

UNIT 3
RIDING HIGH

In the third unit, "Riding High," science is the central theme. It is treated in fiction, essay, poetry, biography, and even folk tale.

Many of today's realities in science began as far-out ideas in the pages of science fiction. As pupils read the highly imaginative selection, "The Television-Chocolate Room" by Roald Dahl, they can speculate on future inventions. The reader does not object to the unlikely fate of Mike Teavee, since he is given only one identifying characteristic—Mike watches TV all day.

As pupils have more and more experience with literature, they come to expect a contemporary, realistic story to be entertaining, to relate to their own lives, to enable them to see themselves as getting along without adults, and to present imaginary experiences possible in real life. "One for the Univac" by Ethelyn M. Parkinson meets all of these expectations.

Essays are one of the most direct ways of presenting scientific information. In "What Television Is" by Jeanne and Robert Bendick technical information is presented. The authors describe live, taped, and filmed programs as well as the relaying of signals by stations and communications satellites. In "Computers in Our World" by Alfred Lewis the author gives specific information on what a computer does and the kinds of questions it can answer. The short photo essay "Man on the Moon" treats the *Apollo 11* spaceflight.

In the poem "Earth, Moon, and Sun" Claudia Lewis translates scientific facts into the world of the poet without sacrificing accuracy. Profound ideas are stated with a minimum of words. Pupils will read this poem quickly and easily, but for full comprehension thought must be focused on the meaning of each word and on concepts hinted at by the use of that word. In "Blue" Claudia Lewis describes what this word means to people on earth in contrast to what it means to the returning astronauts. "The Cloud-Mobile" by May Swenson establishes clouds as maps and models of time.

Biography can offer a source for locating factual information. How the early rockets operated on liquid fuel is described in "Robert H. Goddard: Father of the Space Age" by Clyde B. Moore. Through the study of this biographical sketch pupils can appreciate that spectacular events do not happen spontaneously, but are the result of much planning, experimentation, evaluation, and perseverance.

In Alfred Slote's "By the Light of the Moon" the reader discovers a literary selection that has another genre, or kind, of literature embedded within it. This selection is an essay that includes a folktale from East Africa, explaining the origin of the moon and its phases.

Some of these selections are taken from longer works. Pupils may want to read some of these longer works. Their titles can be found on the Acknowledgments page of *Freedom's Ground* and in the *Teacher's Edition* lesson that accompanies each selection.

The Enrichment Program

While THE HOLT BASIC READING SYSTEM provides within the basic texts and Teacher's Editions a complete program for teaching reading, the authors realize that many teachers use varied enrichment items to accommodate individual needs and differences. Accordingly, an assortment of such items has been especially prepared to accompany "Riding High," Unit 3 in *Freedom's Ground.* The central purpose of all these materials, whatever the media, is to establish models for teachers. These models derive from the basic text and specifically lead to individualization in reinforcing reading skills (Satellite Books), listening skills (recordings), and cognitive and decoding skills (concept and language sound filmstrips). All of these offerings are significant in that imaginative and creative approaches dominate them. Filmstrips and recordings for the entire book are available in *Holt A-V Kit 14.*

SATELLITE BOOKS

Spaceship Earth: Danger! Danger! Danger? by Kenneth and Josephine Sopis

Ecologists are studying problems of pollution; this book realistically lists the pollution dangers around us. Our earth depends on a balance within nature. The authors explain the self-cleaning processes of water, air, and soil and the way man is interfering with these processes. Most important, they offer the reader practical suggestions for helping to eliminate pollution. Text and illustrations, both, emphasize the importance of this timely topic. This book is appropriate for the slower group.

Once pupils have read the biography of Robert H. Goddard and have considered his rocket invention and the ecological problems it presents, they will be ready for this book. A follow-up study card has readers reflect on the question of whether or not the space program will help or hinder the ecology program. The card then suggests that pupils develop advertisements for the ecology cause and create science-fiction stories or posters around the theme of pollution or ecology.

The Adventure of Flight by Joseph Phelan

Have you ever wondered how man conquered seemingly insurmountable problems when he learned to fly? Mr. Phelan traces the history of flying from the time of the Greek myth about Icarus to the present-day supersonic transport planes. He tells of the roles played by Leonardo da Vinci, the Wright Brothers, Lindbergh, and other men. He also traces the impact of aviation on contemporary social conditions. Excellent illustrations make a technical subject surprisingly clear. While this book is planned for better readers, slower readers will learn much from just looking at the pictures and reading the captions.

The Adventure of Flight, a natural extension of the unit theme, "Riding High," is most effective after pupils have read "Computers in Our World." Both selections deal factually with man and airships. On an accompanying study card, pupils work with questions on man's compulsion to fly and life without airplanes.

RECORDINGS

"Earth, Moon, and Sun," page 215.

This provocative poem, which introduces the unit, is read dramatically against a background of music composed by the distinguished musician, Buryl Red. Through psychedelic overtones, Mr. Red has achieved a feeling for the spatial concepts intrinsic in the poem.

SOUND FILMSTRIPS

How TV Tells the News

The filmstrip should precede the reading of "What Television Is," on page 234. It opens with the visit of a camera crew and a newswriter to the Goodyear blimp in Miami, including spectacular views of the Miami ocean front as seen from the blimp. The development of the material gathered into a network broadcast with Walter Cronkite, with a look at behind-the-scenes CBS broadcasting rooms, is the main story of the filmstrip.

The Computers at the Airport

Use the filmstrip after pupils have completed "Computers in Our World," which begins on page 252. The filmstrip follows a mother and her two children who go to the airport to greet the returning father. While waiting, they meet a computer specialist who shows them specifically how computers are used in various ways to support aviation. Realistic photography, graphic examples, and a feeling of humming airport activity will give pupils an in-depth, though vicarious, experience with one practical use of computerization.

Finding Patterns in Words

This filmstrip continues the exploration of decoding printed words through a look at the principles which underlie the structure of English, an adventure in morphology. Compounds, suffixes, clipped forms, and other techniques of word-making referred to in the text are expanded. Pupils are called on to respond. The filmstrip should be used just before the selection that begins on page 282.

Bibliography

Asimov, Isaac, *The Double Planet*. New York: Abelard-Schuman, Ltd.
The fascinating story of how man has probed the secrets of the earth and the moon began in ancient times and is still unfolding. Included in this book are the most recent findings about oceans, satellites, soft lunar landings, and volcanic activity on the moon.

Beatty, Jerome, *Matthew Looney's Voyage to the Earth*. New York: William R. Scott, Inc.
A moon boy, Matthew, yearns to accompany his uncle to the earth. They find enough of interest on earth to cause them to return in the sequel: *Matthew Looney's Invasion of the Earth*.

Belting, Natalia M., *The Moon Is a Crystal Ball: Unfamiliar Legends of the Stars*. Indianapolis: Bobbs-Merrill Company, Inc.

Dr. Belting has gathered legends of the stars and constellations from many lands and peoples.

Bendick, Jeanne, and Robert Bendick, *Television Works Like This.* New York: McGraw-Hill Book Company.
In language as simple as is consistent with the subject, the authors describe and explain the many facets of television. Index, illustrations, and glossary aid in making clear the complicated processes.

Chamberlain, Joseph Miles, *Planets, Stars, and Space.* Mankato, Minn.: Creative Educational Society.
This valuable introduction to the principles of astronomy contains some discussion of space travel. It is written in nontechnical language and illustrated with excellent photographs.

Dahl, Roald, *James and the Giant Peach.* New York: Alfred A. Knopf, Inc.
A fantasy about James and his peach that grows and grows. He and a number of giant insects cross the ocean in the peach and have many adventures.

David, Heather M., *Wernher von Braun.* New York: G. P. Putnam's Sons.
Children will be interested in this thorough biography of the German-born missile expert who came to the United States in 1945 to work on the space and rocket program.

Dewey, Anne Perkins, *Robert Goddard, Space Pioneer.* Boston: Little, Brown & Co.
The life of the American scientist whose work led to the making of our modern liquid fuel rockets is told in a manner that will appeal to young readers.

Jennings, Gary, *March of the Robots.* New York: Dial Press, Inc.
"Robot" is a twentieth-century word but the idea of manufacturing something to act almost human is centuries old.

Kohn, Bernice, *Computers at Your Service.* Englewood Cliffs, N. J.: Prentice-Hall, Inc.
The author gives the history and working principles of computers and describes computers whose nicknames are Univac, Erma, Audrey, Talos, IBM 701, and IBM 709. She also discusses how they are helping our space program, our armed forces, our business and industry.

Lewis, Claudia, *Poems of Earth and Space.* New York: E. P. Dutton & Company, Inc.
These poems written in free verse reflect the space generation's way of looking at the earth, the sky, the sea, and all that is beyond in space.

Lord, Beman, *Day the Spaceship Landed.* New York: Henry Z. Walck, Inc.
The best time to catch frogs is in the afternoon, when the sun has made them groggy. But one day when Mike went to the swamp after school, instead of frogs he found four spacemen.

Swanson, May, *Poems to Solve.* New York: Charles Scribner's Sons.
After pointing out that more meaning is hidden in poetry than in prose, the author offers first a group of riddle poems in which the subject is not named, and then other verses which contain various hidden elements of significance.

Vorwald, Alan, and Frank Clark, *Computers! From Sand Table to Electronic Brain.* New York: McGraw-Hill Book Co.
The author gives a detailed explanation of computer principle and operation, including memory devices, the use of punch cards, and other technical devices. There are directions for building a simple computer.

UNIT 3

RIDING HIGH

14

15

Unit 3
RIDING HIGH

214

EARTH, MOON, AND SUN

Use the recording of the poem to introduce it.

After using the recording, have the poem read silently. Assign six pupils, one to read each stanza. Then have the class read the last stanza in unison. Relate the last line to the unit title.

Have the pupils refer to pages 14 and 15 in the Table of Contents, noting the names of the stories and the poems in the unit. Note the illustrations and establish the unit theme as one that deals with space and technology.

Have the pupils skim the text, pages 215–285. Turn again to the poem and work with the imagery. Establish the meaning of *galaxy* and have the pupils relate the astronomical images here with work they have done in science.

Earth, Moon, and Sun

While the earth spins on,
Turning, turning
Toward the sun,

The moon floats by
In its circle
In our sky.

And while it floats,
Earth and moon, two in one,
Rush on
With the bright planets
In a ring
Around the sun.

And as they rush
And swing
And turn
The gases of the sun
Swirl
And burn.

And all the while these three,
Swirling sun
And moon
And earth,
Spiral in the galaxy.

Spiral in that great wheel turning
With its billion stars
Sparkling,
Burning;

That starry wheel
Where you and I
Night and day
Are riding high,
Riding high!

Claudia Lewis

215

Claudia Lewis
Miss Lewis is a member of the faculty of the Bank Street College of Education in New York City, where she has taught literature and creative writing since 1943. Born in Corvallis, Oregon, she is a graduate of Reed College. In 1959 she received her Ph. D. from Columbia University. Her books of poetry for children include *When I Go to the Moon* and *Strange Room*.

Indicate that this unit will deal with television, both as fantasy and as fact; with computers as fantasy and as fact; and with space as fantasy and as fact. Establish the notion that there are many ways that we have of seeing things, that an author's point of view determines how he will treat a subject. Ask, "What is a Television-Chocolate Room?"

Pupils may want to read more poems like this one in *Poems of Earth and Space* by Claudia Lewis, from which this selection is taken.

The Television-Chocolate Room (pages 216–233)

SUMMARY

Mike Teavee, a boy who watched television constantly, his family, little Charlie Bucket, and Grandpa Joe entered the brightly lit testing room of Mr. Willy Wonka's mysterious chocolate factory. With the help of Oompa-Loompas (factory workers dressed in protective space suits), Mr. Wonka demonstrated how he could transmit a chocolate bar in the same way an ordinary television image is sent. Mike was seized with the idea of sending an actual human being by television. He rushed in front of the powerful camera and in a blinding flash disappeared. When he reappeared on the television screen, Mike was reduced to only one inch in height. Mr. Wonka intended to put Mike in his gum-stretching machine and then fatten him with Supervitamins, but the Oompa-Loompas interrupted him with a loud song about the dangers of letting children get the television-watching habit.

ABOUT THE AUTHOR

Master of many fictional forms, Roald Dahl was born in Llandaff, South Wales, and served as an RAF wing commander during World War II. He is well known for his short stories and mysteries. He received the Edgar Allan Poe Award and two awards from the Mystery Writers of America. His delightful books for children include *The Gremlins, The Magic Finger, Fantastic Mr. Fox,* and *Charlie and the Chocolate Factory,* from which this selection is adapted. Mr. Dahl, his wife, and four children live in Buckinghamshire, England.

MATERIALS

- Workbook pages 50–53.
- Evaluation Masters for "The Television-Chocolate Room."

HUMAN VALUES

- To develop appreciation of the imaginative possibilities inherent in ordinary experience, such as watching television.
- To develop appreciation and enjoyment of science fiction.
- To promote understanding of our own behavior and emotions by understanding the behavior and emotions of story characters.

OBJECTIVES

The objectives listed below refer to specific skills for which lessons are presented in the Reading and Language section for this story. Many other skills are developed in Word Highlights, Interpretation and Comprehension, and through annotations. After reading the selection and participating in the discussion and activities, pupils should be able to demonstrate the following abilities.

1. To identify prepositional phrases and phrase markers in given sentences.
2. To describe the meaning of idiomatic expressions.
3. To construct antonyms by affixing *un-, im-, in-,* or *dis-* to base words.
4. To demonstrate strategies for decoding multisyllabic words containing two or more letters representing one sound.
5. To identify and describe elements that contribute to the humor of a given selection in terms of exaggeration, idioms taken literally, and absurd statements.

Teaching Strategies

WORD HIGHLIGHTS

1. This story has many words which convey a sense of exaggeration and excess. Some of the words are *brilliant, completely enormous, extraordinary, fantastic, great, mighty, miraculously,* and *tremendous.* Have pupils choose a current household product and write several sentences of advertising copy, using some of the above superlatives from the story. Direct them to clip examples of highly exaggerated advertising copy from magazines and to display them on a bulletin board in the classroom.

2. Read this list of words to the class:

send	stand back	dashed	off and running
go	switch on	here it comes	hurried
stop	rushing	whizzing	jog
			presto

   Have pupils discuss how these words will affect the mood of the story they are about to read. (Answers will vary but should include the fact that these words give a sense of quickness and movement to the story and an aura of excitement and turmoil as well.)

3. Explain that many of the characters in this story talk in clichés. Read these examples from the story:

   > Good heavens!
   > Are you off your rocker?
   > See you later, alligator.
   > What on earth do you mean?
   > Don't mention it, dear lady.
   > I haven't the foggiest idea.
   > They all come out in the wash.

   Use these examples to help pupils define *cliché*. (A *cliché* is a figure of speech, a phrase, or a sentence that is used so often it has become overworked and "tired.") Ask pupils to suggest additional examples.

4. Write on the board the following Glossary words:

audience	**idiotic**
commercial	**loll**
electricity	**overdose**
	tantrum

   Have pupils use each word in a sentence.

INTRODUCING THE SELECTION

All the stories and essays in this unit have something to do with science. You study science in school. It helps you to understand the world you live in—the community of plants and animals; sound, light, and color; and machines and electricity.

Scientists find answers by observing, experimenting, and doing research. Sometimes the answers that were accepted yesterday are proven wrong tomorrow. Scientific knowledge is always changing.

Scientists not only gather information but also use this information to produce new inventions that change the world. In this unit you are going to read about several of these inventions: television, communications satellites, computers, and rockets.

The name of the first story is "The Television-Chocolate Room." How many of you have television sets? What are some of your favorite programs?

Write the word *commercial* on the board.

What is a TV commercial? (An ad for a product.) What other meanings does the word *commercial* have?

What are some of the products that you have seen advertised on TV? How do you suppose sponsors for the same kind of product, for example, soap, make you remember their product? What are some words sponsors use to make their products seem the best? (Accept superlatives such as biggest, best, brightest, strongest.)

GUIDED SILENT READING

If you wish to have this story read in two sittings, pupils may read pages 216–222, and then pages 223–233.

In this story the author endows television with very special powers. As you read, be thinking about how the author feels about television. After you read the story silently, we will talk about whether or not he is a TV fan.

Punctuation Signals
Television-Chocolate. Hyphen joins elements of compound adjective. It is unusual because the elements are apparently unrelated.
"—and only five—" Dashes set off repetition of number for emphasis.

Oompa-Loompa
Rhyme combination was originated by the author. *Oompa* simulates the sound of a tuba in a band; *Loompa* comes close to *lump,* one who closely follows orders. Compare *fuddy-duddy, hocus-pocus, hokey-pokey.*

The Television-Chocolate Room
ROALD DAHL

Five children—and only five—were going to be allowed into Mr. Willy Wonka's chocolate factory. The lucky five and their families would get to see all the mysterious machinery in the factory where the world's most wonderful candy was made.

What happens when these five children meet the famous Mr. Willy Wonka? What happens when they pass through the big factory doors? What happens when they come upon the Oompa-Loompas, the factory workers who throw very tiny shadows on the windows and talk in rhyme? What happens when, one by one, the children disobey Mr. Wonka's orders?

Here is what happens to one of the children, Mike Teavee, a boy who does nothing at home but watch television.

216

INTERPRETATION AND COMPREHENSION

SKIMMING FOR IMPORTANT DETAILS
How do we know that this story is part of a longer story by Roald Dahl? (References are made to five children and their adventures, but this story concerns only one child.) Which of the five does this excerpt focus on? (Mike Teavee; discuss the obvious humor of his last name.)

RECOGNIZING SATIRE
We've talked about how the author seems to feel about television. Can you find examples of his making fun of TV on this page? (In paragraph 1, the exaggerated claim, "the world's most wonderful candy," spoofs advertising techniques; in paragraph 2, the exaggerated repetition of unanswered questions about the factory creates a satiric effect.)

Wonka's Super TV

The Teavee family, together with Charlie Bucket and his Grandpa Joe, stepped out of the elevator into a room so dazzlingly bright and dazzlingly white that they screwed up their eyes in pain and stopped walking. Mr. Wonka handed each of them a pair of dark glasses and said, "Put these on quick! And don't take them off in here whatever you do! This light could blind you!"

As soon as Charlie had his dark glasses on, he was able to look around him in comfort. He saw a long, narrow room. The room was painted white all over. Even the floor was white, and there wasn't a speck of dust anywhere. From high above, huge lamps hung down and bathed the room in a brilliant blue-white light. The room was completely bare except at the far ends. At one of these ends, there was an enormous camera on wheels, and a whole army of Oompa-Loompas was clustering around it, oiling its joints and adjusting its knobs and polishing its great glass lens.

The Oompa-Loompas were all dressed in the most extraordinary way. They were wearing bright-red space suits, complete with helmets and goggles—at least they looked like space suits—and they were working in complete silence. Watching them, Charlie experienced a queer sense of danger. There was something dangerous about this whole business, and the Oompa-Loompas knew it. There was no chattering or

217

"dazzlingly bright and dazzlingly white"
Note close repetition of *dazzlingly* plus rhyme of *bright* and *white*. Repetition and rhyme are stylistic techniques used effectively throughout this story.

Personification
"lamps . . . bathed the room in . . . light." Personification is figurative language in which human abilities are given to abstract qualities or inanimate objects.

extraordinary
From Latin (L) *extra*, outside, plus *ordinem*, order, course. Beyond the usual, very exceptional.

Punctuation Signal
"—at least they looked like space suits—" Dashes enclose parenthetical unit.

"a queer sense of danger"
Foreshadowing creates suspense.

Picture the scene described here. What is the outstanding feature of the room the visitors enter? (Its bright whiteness.) Who will find the exact words in the first paragraph that describe this whiteness? (Dazzling bright and dazzling white.) Have you ever heard phrases like these in television ads? For what products? (Soaps promising cleaner clothes.) Who will read aloud the lines that describe further the whiteness of the room? (Paragraph 2.)

What mechanical device sits at one end of the room? (A camera.) How many of its parts are mentioned? (Four.) Name them. (Wheels, joints, knobs, glass lens.)

Read paragraph 3, ending on the next page, silently. Which lines hint at the adventure that is to befall Mike Teavee? (Lines 6 and 7.)

What do you suppose it is that communicates a sense of danger to Charlie Bucket? (The starkness of the room, the uniforms, silence, and careful movements of the Oompa-Loompas.)

VISUALIZING SETTING; FINDING KEY WORDS

ANTICIPATING OUTCOME

singing among them here, and they moved about over the huge black camera slowly and carefully in their scarlet space suits.

At the other end of the room, about fifty paces away from the camera, a single Oompa-Loompa (also wearing a space suit) was sitting at a black table gazing at the screen of a very large television set.

"Here we go!" cried Mr. Wonka, hopping up and down with excitement. "This is the testing room for my very latest and greatest invention— Television Chocolate!"

"But what *is* Television Chocolate?" asked Mike Teavee.

"Good heavens, child, stop interrupting me!" said Mr. Wonka. "It works by television. I don't like television myself. I suppose it's all right in small doses, but children never seem to be able to take it in small doses. They want to sit there all day long, staring and staring at the screen. . . ."

"That's me!" said Mike Teavee.

"Shut up!" said Mr. Teavee.

"Thank you," said Mr. Wonka. "I shall now tell you how this amazing television set of mine works. But first of all, do you know how ordinary television works? It is very simple. At one end, where the picture is being taken, you have a large camera, and you start photographing something. The photographs are then split up into millions

218

Both Willy Wonka and Mike Teavee are enthusiastic, but for different reasons. Who is the real TV fan? (Mike.) Who will read aloud the lines that express Willy Wonka's feelings about TV? (Paragraph 4.)

Do you find anything peculiar about Willy's attitude? (There is a disparity between his occupation and his attitude toward it.) What does excite Willy Wonka? (Television Chocolate.) Who will find a phrase Willy uses that belongs to the world of the commercial? (Latest and greatest invention.)

Throughout the page, Willy Wonka and Mike carry on a dialogue, but only one of the two characters seems to be listening to the other. Who is paying closer attention to the conversation, Willy or Mike? (Mike.) What impression do you have of Willy Wonka so far? (Answers will vary.)

of tiny little pieces which are so small that you can't see them, and these little pieces are shot out into the sky by electricity. In the sky they go whizzing around all over the place until suddenly they hit the antenna on the roof of some person's house. They then go flashing down the wire that leads right into the back of the television set, and in there they get jiggled and joggled around until at last every single one of those millions of tiny pieces is fitted back into its right place (just like a jigsaw puzzle), and presto!—the photograph appears on the screen. . . ."

"That isn't *exactly* how it works," Mike Teavee said.

"I am a little deaf in my left ear," Mr. Wonka said. "You must forgive me if I don't hear everything you say."

"I said, that isn't *exactly* how it works!" shouted Mike Teavee.

"You're a nice boy," Mr. Wonka said, "but you talk too much. Now then! The very first time I

If you were to give Willy Wonka's lecture to his visitors a serious title, what would it be? (An answer like "How Ordinary Television Works" is acceptable.)

GETTING THE MAIN IDEA

Have pupils describe the step-by-step process by which television works as Willy explains it. Develop a list of about nine points on the board.

ISOLATING STEPS IN A PROCESS

Would you characterize Willy's "ordinary TV" as a complicated scientific invention or a magic trick? (His vivid choice of verb phrases adds to the impression of TV as magical.) Who will find some of these verb phrases? (Split up, shot out into the sky, whizzing around all over the place, hit the antenna, flashing down the wire, get jiggled and joggled around, fitted back.)

NOTING WORD USAGE

Why do you suppose Mike has to repeat his response to Willy's explanation twice? (Pupils should observe that Willy is probably not hard of hearing but unwilling to be criticized or contradicted.)

MAKING AN INFERENCE

tremendous
From L *tremere,* to tremble, be afraid
of. Relate *tremor, tremendous, trem-
bling.* Originally that which was *tremendous* caused fear.

Punctuation Signal
"one end of the room to the other—
by television!" Dash reinforces emphasis achieved at end of sentence.
Typical device of advertising rhetoric.
Compare paragraph 7, page 222.

"about the size of the mattress"
Realistic comparison.

saw ordinary television working, I was struck by
a tremendous idea. 'Look here!' I shouted, 'if
these people can break up a *photograph* into
millions of pieces and send the pieces whizzing
through the air and then put them together again
at the other end, why can't *I* do the same thing
with a bar of chocolate? Why can't *I* send a bar
of chocolate whizzing through the air in tiny
pieces and then put the pieces together at the
other end, all ready to be eaten?'"

"Impossible!" said Mike Teavee.

"You think so?" cried Mr. Wonka. "Well, watch
this! I shall now send a bar of my very best chocolate from one end of the room to the other—by
television! Get ready, over there! Bring in the
chocolate!"

Immediately six Oompa-Loompas marched
forward carrying on their shoulders the most
enormous bar of chocolate Charlie had ever seen.
It was about the size of the mattress he slept on
at home.

"It has to be big," Mr. Wonka explained, "because whenever you send something by television,

220

THINKING CRITICALLY   Who will read aloud the thinking that leads to Willy Wonka's latest invention?
(Top of page.) If you hadn't finished reading the story, what would you now
think of the chances of Willy's success with such an idea? Why? Can you
find anything seriously wrong with his logic? (If necessary, guide pupils to see
that his reasoning is faulty: in ordinary television, the original source of the
image remains intact after it has been transmitted electronically. A picture is
taken of the object, and this picture is sent by television. The object itself is
not sent.)

it always comes out much smaller than it was when it went in. Even with *ordinary* television, if you photograph a big man, he never comes out on your screen any taller than a pencil, does he? Here we go, then! Get ready! *No, no! Stop! Hold everything!* You there! Mike Teavee! Stand back! You're too close to the camera! There are dangerous rays coming out of that thing! They could break you up into a million tiny pieces in one second! That's why the Oompa-Loompas are wearing space suits! The suits protect them! All right! That's better! Now, then! *Switch on!*"

One of the Oompa-Loompas caught hold of a large switch and pulled it down. Then there was a blinding flash.

"The chocolate's gone!" shouted Grandpa Joe, waving his arms.

He was quite right! The whole enormous bar of chocolate had disappeared completely into thin air.

"It's on its way!" cried Mr. Wonka. "It is now rushing through the air above our heads in a million tiny pieces. Quick! Come over here!" He dashed over to the other end of the room where the large television set was standing, and the others followed him. "Watch the screen!" he cried. "Here it comes! Look!"

The screen flickered and lit up. Then suddenly a small bar of chocolate appeared in the middle of the screen.

221

Slang
"Hold everything!"

Idiom
"disappeared . . . into thin air." Idiom is a phrase whose total meaning cannot be derived literally from each word, or a phrase with special grammatical usage.

"It's on its way!"
It's is a contraction; *its* is a possessive.

"small bar of chocolate"
Note continuing contrast between large and small, enormous and tiny, a million and one. These disparities highlight the extremes of television itself.

Pupils' attention should be directed to the absurdity in the idea of sending a mattress-sized chocolate bar: the size of the image on the TV screen depends on the size of the screen, not on the size of the original object sent.

RECOGNIZING ABSURDITY

How can we tell in the section at the top of the page that Willy is upset? (From his short, emphatic sentences, punctuated by exclamation points.) Who will read his excited speech aloud?

RECOGNIZING STYLE

What sentences prove that anything can happen in fiction? (Paragraphs 2 and 3.) In the third paragraph, the author uses exaggeration to emphasize the importance of the event that has just occurred. Who can rephrase the sentence that begins with the words, "The whole . . ." so that there are no unnecessary words in it? (The words *whole, enormous, completely,* and *into thin air* can be dropped without changing the sentence's essential meaning.)

DISTINGUISHING BETWEEN STATEMENT AND OVERSTATEMENT

miracle, miraculously
From L *mirari*, to wonder at, be astonished. Relate *admire*, *mirage*, *mirror*, *admiration*, *marvel*, and *marvelous*.

"It's . . . it's . . . it's"
Ellipses and repetition reflect speechless wonder. Ellipses in next paragraph signify a dreamy pause.

Punctuation Signal
"'Eat Wonka's Chocolates! . . . now!'" Note use of single quotation marks within quotation.

"Take it!" shouted Mr. Wonka, growing more and more excited.

"How can you take it?" asked Mike Teavee, laughing. "It's just a picture on a television screen!"

"Charlie Bucket!" cried Mr. Wonka. "*You* take it! Reach out and grab it!"

Charlie put out his hand and touched the screen, and suddenly, miraculously, the bar of chocolate came away in his fingers. He was so surprised, he nearly dropped it.

"Eat it!" shouted Mr. Wonka. "Go on and eat it! It'll be delicious! It's the same bar! It's gotten smaller on the journey, that's all!"

"It's absolutely fantastic!" gasped Grandpa Joe. "It's . . . it's . . . it's a miracle!"

"Just imagine," cried Mr. Wonka, "when I start using this across the country . . . you'll be sitting at home watching television, and suddenly a commercial will flash onto the screen, and a voice will say, 'Eat Wonka's Chocolates! They're the best in the world! If you don't believe us, try one for yourself—*now!*' And you simply reach out and take one! How about that, eh?"

"Terrific!" cried Grandpa Joe. "It will change the world!"

RECOGNIZING PLOT DEVELOPMENT	What happens on this page that affects the rest of the story? (Willy Wonka succeeds in sending a chocolate bar through a TV set.)
FINDING KEY WORDS	If we hadn't noticed how amazing the results of Willy's experiment were, which word in the fourth paragraph tells us? (Miraculous.) What other words are used on the page to express astonishment at what happened? (Fantastic, miracle, terrific.)
RECOGNIZING ABSURDITY	Willy dreams of future successes. Who will read aloud his dramatic words? (Paragraph 7.) Is there anything wrong with his plan? (Pupils may observe that there might be a problem involved in transmitting one chocolate bar into millions of homes.)
DRAWING A CONCLUSION	Do you agree with Grandpa Joe's last statement? (Answers will vary.)

Some Very Nasty Results

Mike Teavee was even more excited than Grandpa Joe at seeing a bar of chocolate being sent by television. "But Mr. Wonka," he shouted, "can you send *other things* through the air in the same way? Breakfast cereal, for instance?"

"Oh, my sainted aunt!" cried Mr. Wonka. "Don't mention that disgusting stuff in front of me! It's made of those little curly wooden shavings you find in pencil sharpeners!"

"But could you send it by television if you wanted to, as you do chocolate?" asked Mike Teavee.

"Of course I could!"

"And what about people?" asked Mike Teavee. "Could you send a real live person from one place to another in the same way?"

"A *person!*" cried Mr. Wonka. "Are you off your rocker?"

"But *could* it be done?"

"Good heavens, child, I really don't know . . . I suppose it *could* be done . . . yes, I'm pretty sure it could . . . of course it could . . . I wouldn't like to risk it, though . . . it might have some very nasty results. . . ."

But Mike Teavee was already off and running. The moment he heard Mr. Wonka saying, "Yes, I'm pretty sure it could . . . of course it could," he turned away and started running as fast as he could towards the other end of the room where

Slang
"Oh, my sainted aunt!"
"Are you off your rocker?"
"Off your rocker" means crazy, with image taken from a rocking chair.

Punctuation Signal
"I really don't know . . . ." Repeated use of ellipses denotes the hestitation while Mr. Wonka is thinking aloud.

nasty
Used frequently in British English— a form of understatement for *dangerous, grave.*

"off and running"
Racing phrase.

223

Why do you suppose Mike Teavee is more excited than Grandpa Joe? (Mike is the TV buff; pupils can speculate about whether Mike has in mind sending himself over TV when he asks about breakfast cereal.)

Who will read aloud the lines that for the first time reveal Willy in a state of uncertainty? (Paragraph 8.)

Does Mike run toward the TV camera before, during, or after the time Willy answers his question about sending a person over TV? (During.) Who will find the lines that prove your answer? (Paragraph 9.)

UNDERSTANDING CHARACTERS

RECOGNIZING TIME RELATIONSHIPS

the great camera was standing. "Look at me!" he shouted as he ran. "I'm going to be the first person in the world to be sent by television!"

"*No, no, no, no!*" cried Mr. Wonka.

"Mike!" screamed Mrs. Teavee. "Stop! Come back! You'll be turned into a million tiny pieces!"

But there was no stopping Mike Teavee now. The crazy boy rushed on, and when he reached the enormous camera, he jumped straight for the switch, scattering Oompa-Loompas right and left as he went.

"See you later, alligator!" Mike shouted, and he pulled down the switch. As he did so, he leaped out into the full glare of the mighty lens.

There was a blinding flash.

Then there was silence.

Then Mrs. Teavee ran forward . . . but she stopped dead in the middle of the room . . . and she stood there . . . she stood staring at the place where her son had been . . . and her great red mouth opened wide, and she screamed. "He's gone! He's gone!"

"Great heavens, he *has* gone!" shouted Mr. Teavee.

RECOGNIZING PLOT DEVELOPMENT — Things suddenly are happening fast. What happens here that affects the outcome of the story? (Mike sends himself by television.)

SKIMMING FOR SPECIFIC INFORMATION — Who will find and read aloud Mrs. Teavee's warning shout? (Paragraph 2.) The sentences describing the height of the action? (Paragraphs 3 through 6.) Mrs. Teavee's frightening discovery? (Paragraph 7.)

UNDERSTANDING DESCRIPTION — Why is she described as having a "great red mouth"? (It represents her screaming hysteria.)

225

What are the Oompa-Loompas doing in the picture on this page? (They are running away from the camera.) What is happening to Mike? (He is caught in a blinding flash of light.)

USING PICTURE CLUES

"Mr. and Mrs. Teavee and Grandpa Joe . . . ."
Repetition of *and* simulates juvenile style of enumeration. The simple statement, ''The screen was quite blank,'' comes as an anticlimax.

Colloquialism
''What on earth . . .?''

alarm
From L *ad illam,* to that, plus *arma,* weapons. A call to arms or warning of danger. Relate *alarmist.*

Mr. Wonka hurried forward and placed a hand gently on Mrs. Teavee's shoulder. "We shall have to hope for the best," he said. "We must pray that your little boy will come out unharmed at the other end."

"Mike!" screamed Mrs. Teavee, clasping her head in her hands. "Where are you?"

"I'll tell you where he is," said Mr. Teavee, "he's whizzing around above our heads in a million tiny pieces!"

"Don't talk about it!" wailed Mrs. Teavee.

"We must watch the television set," said Mr. Wonka. "He may come through any moment."

Mr. and Mrs. Teavee and Grandpa Joe and little Charlie and Mr. Wonka all gathered round the television and stared tensely at the screen. The screen was quite blank.

"He's taking a long time to come across," said Mr. Teavee, wiping his brow.

"Oh dear, oh dear," said Mr. Wonka, "I do hope that no part of him gets left behind."

"What on earth do you mean?" asked Mr. Teavee sharply.

"I don't wish to alarm you," said Mr. Wonka, "but it does sometimes happen that only about

226

INTERPRETING GESTURES

As we've noticed before, characters often reveal their feelings not through dialogue but through gestures. Skim this page. Who will locate gestures made by various characters and tell us what emotions they are expressing? (Paragraph 1: Willy places a hand gently on Mrs. Teavee's shoulder, gesture indicates compassion; paragraph 2: Mrs. Teavee clasps her head in her hands, gesture shows she is grief-stricken; paragraph 7: Mr. Teavee wipes his brow, gesture indicates anxiety.)

USING PICTURE CLUES

What can you tell about the reactions of the characters from the pictures on this page and the next? (They are excited.)

IDENTIFYING WITH A CHARACTER

What do you imagine Mike was thinking as he jumped in front of the camera? Which possibilities didn't he consider? (Answers will vary.)

half the little pieces find their way into the television set. It happened last week. I don't know why, but the result was that only half a bar of chocolate came through."

Mrs. Teavee let out a scream of horror. "You mean only a half of Mike is coming back to us?" she cried.

"Let's hope it's the top half," said Mr. Teavee.

"Hold everything!" said Mr. Wonka. "Watch the screen! Something's happening!"

The screen had suddenly begun to flicker.

Then some wavy lines appeared.

Mr. Wonka adjusted one of the knobs, and the wavy lines went away.

And now, very slowly, the screen began to get brighter and brighter.

"Here he comes!" yelled Mr. Wonka. "Yes, that's him all right!"

"Is he all in one piece?" cried Mrs. Teavee.

"I'm not sure," said Mr. Wonka. "It's too early to tell."

Faintly at first, but becoming clearer and clearer every second, the picture of Mike appeared on the screen. He was standing up and waving at the audience and grinning.

Colloquialism
"Yes, that's him all right!"

227

After a new machine has been invented or a new medicine has been discovered, why isn't it made available to the public for a while? (Pupils should consider the need for testing and experimentation in order to ensure the reliability of these products before they are released to the public.) What is the flaw in Willy Wonka's invention so far? (Top of page.)

THINKING BEYOND TEXT

How do you feel about Mr. Teavee's reaction to Willy's terrible announcement? (Pupils should detect the humor in his response.)

APPRECIATING HUMOR

To offer pupils practice in organizing information in sequential order, write on the board the following steps involved in the process of Mike's reappearance; have pupils reorder them in proper sequence: 1) Screen gets brighter. 2) Wavy lines appear. 3) Picture of Mike appears clearer and clearer. 4) Screen flickers. 5) Willy Wonka adjusts knobs. 6) Faint picture of Mike appears. The correct sequence is 4, 2, 5, 1, 6, and 3.

NOTING CORRECT SEQUENCE

"But he's a midget!" shouted Mr. Teavee.

"Mike," cried Mrs. Teavee, "are you all right? Are there any bits of you missing?"

"Isn't he going to get any bigger?" shouted Mr. Teavee.

"Talk to me, Mike!" cried Mrs. Teavee. "Say something! Tell me you're all right!"

A tiny little voice, no louder than the squeaking of a mouse, came out of the television set. "Hi, Mum!" it said. "Hi, Pop! Look at *me!* I'm the first person ever to be sent by television!"

"Grab him!" ordered Mr. Wonka. "Quick!"

Mrs. Teavee shot out a hand and very carefully picked the tiny figure of Mike Teavee out of the screen.

"Hooray!" cried Mr. Wonka. "He's all in one piece! He's completely unharmed!"

"You call *that* unharmed?" snapped Mrs. Teavee, peering at the little speck of a boy who was now running to and fro across the palm of her hand, waving his pistols in the air.

He was certainly not more than an inch tall.

"He's *shrunk!*" said Mr. Teavee.

"Of course, he's shrunk," said Mr. Wonka. "What did you expect?"

"This is terrible!" wailed Mrs. Teavee. "What *are* we going to do?"

UNDERSTANDING CHARACTERS

In what condition does Mike finally appear? (As a midget.) How does Mrs. Teavee react to Mike's appearance? (Paragraphs 1, 4, 7, 9, and 13.)

Do you suppose it would be fair to say that Willy Wonka is more interested in machines than he is in human beings? Give reasons for your answer. (Yes, Willy is unconcerned with Mike's altered condition. Earlier in the story, he demonstrated insensitivity to people's feelings.)

IDENTIFYING WITH A CHARACTER

Pupils might enjoy fantasizing that they are shrinking down to one inch. Have each of them describe how he imagines he would feel and how his experience of things would change if he became so tiny.

And Mr. Teavee said, "We can't send him back to school like this! He'll get trod upon! He'll get squashed!"

"He won't be able to do *anything!*" cried Mrs. Teavee.

"Oh, yes I will!" squeaked the tiny voice of Mike Teavee. "I can still watch television!"

"Never again!" shouted Mr. Teavee. "I'm throwing the television set right out the window the moment we get home. I've had enough of television!"

When he heard this, Mike Teavee flew into a terrible tantrum. He started jumping up and down on the palm of his mother's hand, screaming and trying to bite her fingers. "I want to watch television!" he squeaked. "I want to watch television! I want to watch television!"

"Here! Give him to me!" said Mr. Teavee, and he took the tiny boy and shoved him into the breast pocket of his jacket and stuffed a handkerchief on top. Squeals and yells came from inside the pocket, and the pocket shook as the furious little prisoner fought to get out.

"Oh, Mr. Wonka," wailed Mrs. Teavee, "how can we make him grow?"

"Well," said Mr. Wonka, rubbing his chin and gazing thoughtfully at the ceiling, "I must say

Alliteration
"terrible tantrum"
"I want to watch television!"
"furious little prisoner fought"

229

Tempers reach a high point among the Teavees. Why does Mr. Teavee lose his temper? (Paragraph 4.) Mike? (Paragraph 5.) How does Mr. Teavee stifle Mike's screams? (Paragraph 6.)

INTERPRETING EMOTIONS

Have the parts of each character on this page read aloud dramatically.

DRAMATIZING DIALOGUE

that's a wee bit tricky. But small boys are extremely springy and elastic. They stretch like mad. So what we'll do, we'll put him in a special machine I have for testing the stretchiness of chewing gum! Maybe that will bring him back to what he was."

"Oh, thank you!" said Mrs. Teavee.

"Don't mention it, dear lady."

"How far d'you think he'll stretch?" asked Mr. Teavee.

"Maybe miles," said Mr. Wonka. "Who knows? But he's going to be awfully thin. Everything gets thinner when you stretch it."

"You mean like chewing gum?" asked Mr. Teavee.

"Exactly."

"Just how thin will he be?" asked Mrs. Teavee anxiously.

"I haven't the foggiest idea," said Mr. Wonka. "And it doesn't really matter, anyway, because we'll soon fatten him up again. All we'll have to do is give him a triple overdose of my wonderful Supervitamin Candy. Supervitamin Candy contains huge amounts of vitamin A and vitamin B. It also contains vitamin C, vitamin D, vitamin E, vitamin F, vitamin G, vitamin I, vitamin J, vitamin K, vitamin L, vitamin M, vitamin N, vitamin O, vitamin P, vitamin Q, vitamin R, vitamin T, vitamin U, vitamin V, vitamin W, vitamin X, vitamin Y, *and*, believe it or not, vitamin Z!

230

RECOGNIZING SYNONYMS

Pondering a solution to Mike's problem, Willy Wonka makes an observation about boys. Who will find two synonyms he uses to describe them? (Springy, elastic.) What do these words suggest to you? (Pupils should understand that they indicate a general flexibility.) What does Willy mean by these words? (He has their strictly literal meaning in mind.)

GETTING MAIN IDEAS; MAKING A JUDGMENT

What is Willy's two-fold answer to Mike's problem? (Top of page and paragraph 8.) Even if Willy's plan works, has he considered everything? (No, Mike may wind up giant-sized.)

RECOGNIZING SATIRE

Call for pupils' responses to the final paragraph. Guide them to appreciate the author's satiric intent: he mocks over-reliance on pills and the sweeping claims that are often made for various products. Have pupils distinguish between actual and nonsense vitamins; explain that in reality the human body will reject, not absorb, an overdose of vitamin pills.

The only two vitamins it doesn't have in it are vitamin S, because it makes you sick, and vitamin H, because it makes you grow horns out of the top of your head, like a bull. But it *does* have in it a very small amount of the rarest and most magical vitamin of them all—vitamin Wonka."

"And what will *that* do to him?" asked Mr. Teavee anxiously.

"It'll make his toes grow out until they're as long as his fingers. . . ."

"Oh, no!" cried Mrs. Teavee.

"Don't be silly," said Mr. Wonka. "It's most useful. He'll be able to play the piano with his feet."

"But, Mr. Wonka . . ."

"No arguments, *please!*" said Mr. Wonka. He turned away and clicked his fingers three times in the air. An Oompa-Loompa appeared immediately and stood beside him. "Follow these orders," said Mr. Wonka, handing the Oompa-Loompa a piece of paper on which he had written full instructions. "And you'll find the boy in his father's pocket. Off you go! Good-by, Mr. Teavee! Good-by, Mrs. Teavee! And please don't look so worried! They all come out in the wash, you know, every one of them. . . ."

At the end of the room, the Oompa-Loompas around the giant camera were already beating their tiny drums and beginning to jog up and down to the rhythm.

231

"it makes you sick, . . . makes you grow horns. . . ."
Typical use of *you* as in phrases for selling various products.

Punctuation Signal
"—vitamin Wonka." Dash marks emphatic pause before product name.

Idiom
"They all come out in the wash . . ."

How do you think Willy Wonka chooses the letters for the vitamins that go into his Supervitamin Candy? (The letters seem to stand for qualities or powers the vitamins possess; clarify the fact that the letter names of real vitamins have no meaning.)

MAKING AN INFERENCE

Write the name *Willy Wonka* on the board. Under the name list these traits: self-importance, indifference to people's feelings, bossiness, kindliness. Choose pupils to read aloud the lines on this page that show each quality in Willy's personality.

UNDERSTANDING A CHARACTER

Punctuation Signal
"Them near your television set—"
Dash used like a semicolon preceding
a second independent thought.

Overstatement
"A dozen eyeballs"

"There they go again!" said Mr. Wonka. "I'm
afraid you can't stop them singing."

Little Charlie caught Grandpa Joe's hand, and
the two of them stood beside Mr. Wonka as they
listened to the Oompa-Loompas sing. And this is
what they sang.

"The most important thing we've learned
So far as children are concerned,
Is *never*, NEVER, NEVER let
Them near your television set—
Or better still, just don't install
The idiotic thing at all.
In almost every house we've been,
We've watched them gaping at the screen.
They loll and slop and lounge about,
And stare until their eyes pop out.
(Last week in someone's place we saw
A dozen eyeballs on the floor.)

• • •

'All right!' you'll cry. 'All right!' you'll say,
'But if we take the set away,
What shall we do to entertain
Our darling children? Please explain!'
We'll answer this by asking you,
'What *used* the darling ones to do?
How *used* they keep themselves contented
Before this monster was invented?
Have you forgotten? Don't you know?'

GETTING THE MAIN IDEAS

Silently reread the song of the Oompa-Loompas that ends on the next page.
What is the lesson, or moral, of the verse? (Children and TV don't mix well.)
What angry words are used to describe TV? (The idiotic thing, this monster.)
Based on its appearance, can you make up other disapproving terms for TV?
(Answers will vary.) What two main objections are raised to TV viewing?
(Children spend too much time watching it, and it takes them away from a
more valuable activity, reading.) Can you think of any advantages that a TV
set has over a book? a book over a TV set?

CHOOSING RELEVANT DETAILS

MAKING JUDGMENTS

RELATING READING TO
EXPERIENCE

Do any of you spend all your spare time watching TV? What are some of your
other favorite activities?

UNDERSTANDING POETIC
EFFECTS

Focus attention on the rhyming couplets and the choice of verbs in lines 8,
9, and 10, suggesting passivity.

We'll say this very loud and slow:
'They . . . used . . . to . . . READ! They'd *read*
   and *read,*
And read and *read,* and then proceed
To *read* some more. Great Scott! Gadzooks!
One half their lives was reading books!'

      • • •

P.S. Regarding Mike Teavee,
We very much regret that we
Shall simply have to wait and see
If we can get him back his height.
But if we can't—it serves him right."

Reflections

1. What was wrong with Mr. Wonka's explanation of how "ordinary" television works? (If you don't know, consult an encyclopedia.)
2. Mr. Wonka was clever enough to invent his amazing television set, but do you think a person could carry on an intelligent discussion with him? Give evidence from the story to support your opinion.
3. What is your opinion of boys and girls who watch television all day?
4. Suppose that manufacturers *could* send samples of their products into private homes by television. Do you think that would be good or bad? First take one side of the question, then the other.
5. In this story, Mike seems to be a bright (though troublesome) boy. Perhaps he could have figured out a way to get back to his normal size himself. What ideas might you suggest for him to try? Make up a story in which he uses one or more of these ideas.

233

Punctuation Signals
"We'll say this very loud and slow:"
Colon signals message to follow.

"But if we can't—" Dash again used to indicate pause before the final climax.

" 'They . . . used . . . to . . . READ!' "
Ellipses indicate the measured manner in which these words were spoken.

P.S.
Abbreviation for L *post-*, after, plus *scribere*, to write.

Idiom
"it serves him right." *Serves* here has the special meaning of being paid or requited; hence the meaning, "he is paid as he deserves."

After pupils have gone over the verse once or twice, have the verse read in a chorus.

Have pupils skim through the story to locate all unrealistic elements. Such elements should include the powers of the television camera and set, the Oompa-Loompas, the Supervitamin Candy, the shrinking of Mike Teavee, the scheme for stretching him, and the zany attitudes of the characters in the story. Then have them find words that exaggerate. They might suggest such words as *amazing, extraordinary, latest, terrific, super, brilliant, absolutely, delicious, enormous, presto, miracle, greatest,* and *results.* Then have pupils use these words in creating their own ads to sell imaginary products.

RECOGNIZING UNREALISTIC ELEMENTS

FINDING KEY WORDS

RELATING READING TO EXPERIENCE

Suggest that pupils may want to read more about this subject in *Charlie and the Chocolate Factory* by Roald Dahl.

Questions 3–5 can be used as the basis for group discussion. Question 1 is a good research question. Question 2 focuses on characterization.

USING REFLECTIONS

READING AND LANGUAGE

I. READING SKILLS

● **To identify prepositional phrases and phrase markers in given sentences. (Syntax)**

To introduce the prepositional phrase to the group, write the following sentence on the board and have it read.

> The Teavee family arrived there early.

How could we make this sentence tell in greater detail where the Teavee family was going? (Substitute *at the factory* for *there*.) We can change this sentence again to make it still more informative. What time did the family arrive? Let's substitute *at eight o'clock* for the word *early*. Similar phrases, or word groups, in sentences give us many details as we read.

Write the prepositions below on the board and tell pupils these prepositions often signal the start of a word group or phrase in a sentence. Therefore, we call them *phrase markers*. Ask pupils to read page 219 and see how many of these words they can find.

in	above	at	with
into	across	before	on
of	by	after	outside
through	under	inside	around

You can see that a noun is the last word in such phrases. What other kinds of words make up these word groups besides the prepositions at the beginning and the nouns at the end? (Noun markers, adjectives.)

Write the following sentences on the board or duplicate them. Ask pupils to draw a line under the prepositional phrases. Then have the sentences read aloud and the prepositional phrase identified.

1. Mike Teavee jumped before the camera.

2. A tiny Mike appeared on the screen.

3. It works by electricity.

4. You're too close to the camera.

5. His father put Mike inside his pocket.

Grouping the words that make up prepositional phrases
T•390 can help you to become a better reader.

● **To describe the meaning of idiomatic expressions. (Semantics)**

You have probably used the expression "How do you do?" Look at the words in this sentence and define them. Literally, what does the sentence mean? (Answers will vary; actually, it is nonsense if taken literally.) What do we mean when we use this expression? (How are you? Greetings. Hello.) Who knows what this type of expression is called? (An idiom. Write the term on the board.)

We use many other expressions that cannot be understood from the ordinary meanings of the individual words in them. Who can think of some others? (Suggestions: I caught a cold; I give up; he took over the business; I will look over the papers; he will take up golf.)

Present the following practice exercise.

Here are some idiomatic expressions from the story. Write a short explanation of each one.

1. They screwed up their eyes.
   The light made their eyes squint.

2. . . . grinning from ear to ear.
   very happy, big smile

3. Mike Teavee flew into a terrible rage.
   He became very angry.

4. I was struck by a tremendous idea.
   I thought of a great idea.

5. Are you off your rocker?
   Are you crazy?

● **To construct antonyms by affixing un-, im-, in-, or dis- to base words. (Morphology)**

Write the following prefixes and words on the board.

1. un-		3. in-	
2. im-		4. dis-	

1	happy	4	loyal	3	efficient	2	prudent
4	please	3	action	1	harmed	2	mature

Who will give us a meaning common to all the prefixes on the board? (Not.) Antonyms, or words meaning the opposite, can sometimes be made by adding negative prefixes. For example, by adding the prefixes *un-, im-, in-,* or *dis-,* we can form clear antonyms: *happy—unhappy, loyal—disloyal, efficient—inefficient,* etc.

Write these sentences on the board. Have the sentences read aloud rapidly to convey the excitement of the scene from the story.

> Mr. Wonka cried, "He's all in one piece! He's completely not harmed!"
> Mr. Wonka cried, "He's all in one piece! He's completely unharmed!"

Is it difficult to say the *h* in *harm* when it followed the *t* in *not?* (Yes.) Was it easier to say the *h* in *harm* when it followed the prefix *un-?* (Probably.)

Study the words on the board in the first three columns. How do you know which "not" prefix to use before each of these words? (Sounds right, familiar, check dictionary.) Turn to the prefix *im-* in your dictionaries. What does it mean? (*Im-* is used for *in-* before *b, m,* or *p.*) Who remembers what *in-* means? (Not.) *Ir-* is another form of the negative prefix *in-.* It is used before words beginning with *r,* such as *responsible—irresponsible.*

Have pupils match the numbers of the prefixes with the base words, and use the new words in oral sentences.

OBJECTIVE 4

● **To demonstrate strategies for decoding multisyllabic words containing two or more letters representing one sound. (Phonology)**

Duplicate or write the following words on the board, and underline the double consonants.

dazzling	tissue
intelligent	antenna
terrible	beginning

Say each word to yourself. How many consonant sounds do the underlined letters stand for? (One.) Now say the words again and tell us which syllable is stressed. (The one that contains the double consonant.) What kind of vowel sound do you hear in the syllable with primary stress? ("Short," or unglided.) Why? (The syllable ends in two consonants standing for one sound; the syllable pattern is CVC.)

Who can state a general rule for decoding, or pronouncing, words with double consonants? (When double consonants are in the middle of a word, divide after them for pronunciation and put primary stress on the syllable they are in. The vowel sound in that syllable is usually short.)

Note that exceptions to the stress pattern and syllable division may occur, as in *terrif'ic* and in compounds such as *cattail,* where syllable division is based on the separate words, and in affixed words such as *appear,* where division is based on affix plus root. Pupils may add to the list as many story words with double consonants as they can find.

Write on the board the following list of words, and proceed as with the previous list of words with double consonants.

flashing	gather
flicker	earthen
singer	teacher
graphic	matching

Have pupils state the general rule for decoding words with two or more consonant letters standing for one consonant sound. Exceptions to the division or stress pattern may occur, as in *machine'* and in words of more than two syllables such as *mathematics.*

Similar lists of words may be presented with two or more vowel letters representing one vowel sound, such as *reason, beautiful, screening.* Pupils should note that the vowel sounds are "long," or glided and that primary stress is on the syllable with the glided sound.

II. LITERARY SKILLS

OBJECTIVE 5

● **To identify and describe elements that contribute to the humor of a given selection, in terms of exaggeration, idioms taken literally, and absurd statements. (Rhetoric)**

Suppose you had been looking forward to watching a television production of "The Television-Chocolate Room." The hour for the program to begin arrives and you find, to your disappointment, that the sound on your TV set isn't working. Do you think that the action of the story would hold your interest even without the sound? What scenes might you find particularly interesting?

Pupils may cite such episodes as Willy Wonka hopping up and down with excitement as he showed his visitors the testing room; Mike Teavee running toward the television camera and jumping for the switch; Mrs. Teavee opening her great red mouth; tiny Mike running to and fro in his mother's palm, waving his pistols in the air and having a tantrum; and the Oompa-Loompas beating their drums and jogging.

Action can be very funny. But suppose the sound is suddenly restored. Now you will be able to appreciate the humor of the story much more fully. The author makes fun of certain things. What are they? (Television, television viewers, sponsors, advertising techniques with exaggerated claims.) Some of the humor comes to us from the language the author uses to tell the story and some comes from the dialogue between characters.

The following exercise may be presented orally. Write on the board three lettered reasons behind the humor of this selection. As you read each situation aloud, have pupils select the reason for the humor.

    a. exaggeration
    b. absurdity
    c. idiom taken literally

1. *Page 221:* "It has to be big," Mr. Wonka explained, "because whenever you send something by television, it always comes out much smaller than it was when it went in."   b

2. *Page 223:* "Don't mention that disgusting stuff in front of me. It's made of those little curly shavings you find in pencil sharpeners."   a

3. *Page 227:* Mrs. Teavee let out a scream of horror. "You mean only a half of Mike is coming back to us?" she cried.

"Let's hope it's the top half," said Mrs. Teavee.   b

4. *Page 229:* When he heard this, Mike Teavee flew into a terrible tantrum. He started jumping up and down on the palm of his mother's hand, screaming and trying to bite her fingers. "I want to watch television!" he squeaked.   b

5. *Page 230:* ". . . small boys are extremely springy and elastic. They stretch like mad."   c

6. *Page 231:* "The only two vitamins it doesn't have in it are vitamin S, because it makes you sick, and vitamin H, because it makes you grow horns out of the top of your head, like a bull."   b

7. *Page 232:* They loll and slop and lounge about,
And stare until their eyes pop out.
(Last week in someone's place we saw
A dozen eyeballs on the floor.)   c

III. REGROUPING FOR INDIVIDUAL NEEDS

Reinforcement Activities

The following reteaching activities are suggested for use with pupils who had difficulty with the Evaluation Masters. The teacher should develop additional exercises as needed.

Objective 1: Write on the board the phrase markers listed in the lesson. Have pupils develop each one into a prepositional phrase orally by adding a noun or a determiner and a noun. For example: "in the house." Follow the oral discussion by having the pupils write five sentences using prepositional phrases.

Objective 4: Write on the board the following list of words. Have pupils underline the two consonants that stand for one sound, and tell whether the accented vowel is long or short.

pattern	washing
syllable	sicker
follow	rather

Extension Activities

Objective 5: Pupils may skim the story and make a list of ten statements or actions that they consider funny. Encourage them to compare their lists with each other and attempt to explain why they think these elements are humorous.

IV. ENRICHMENT

- Divide the class into groups in which all members have the same favorite television program. Then direct each group to produce a three- to five-minute sketch which either imitates the show or spoofs it in a humorous way.

  Encourage each different "production company" to use props, such as desks, chairs, and tables, simple sound effects, a program announcer, and an applause sign. The group may want to lampoon one or two well-known commercials as part of its overall presentation.

- Have pupils discuss their own television viewing habits and those of the public at large. Spark the discussion with this question: "Why do you think *(name of a current program)* is one of the most popular television shows of the season?" Lead pupils to discuss why they are attracted to the programs that they consider their favorites.

- Present pupils with this hypothetical situation: "Imagine you are given the chance to be the only person in America directly responsible for what appears on television. Your first job is to give everyone who watches television the opportunity to watch what you think they should watch." Have pupils write a description of what they would like to have everyone watch on television. These may reflect their own preferences for news programs, cartoon shows, sports events, science-fiction shows. Possibilities are endless.

- Have the class discuss the last stanza of the poem on page 233. "What will happen to Mike Teavee? How do the Oompa-Loompas feel about his future? Do you think they are going to try to help him?"

  Divide the class into four groups. Have two groups decide what will happen to Mike if he does not regain his size. Have them consider how he will change, what activities he will be able to participate in, how people will react to him. Have the remaining two groups decide what Mike's attitude may be if he does return to normal size. Have a spokesman for each group tell their ending to the story.

What Television Is (pages 234–239)

SUMMARY

Television enables more people than ever before to see and hear what takes place around the world. Television programs are presented live, on tape, or on film; or they may be a combination of these methods. The techniques of relaying television signals by means of automatic ground stations and by communications satellites are explained in this selection.

ABOUT THE AUTHORS

Jeanne and Robert Bendick collaborated on *Television Works Like This*, the source of this explanatory essay. Jeanne Bendick, a graduate of Parsons School of Design, is an illustrator and has written many books for children dealing with mathematics and technical subjects. Her husband studied engineering and photography. He served in the United States Air Force (1942–45) and is a television cameraman. The Bendicks, who live in Rye, New York, have one son and one daughter.

MATERIALS

- Sound filmstrip *How TV Tells the News.*
- Workbook pages 54–56.
- Evaluation Masters for "What Television Is."

HUMAN VALUES

- To stimulate an interest in the technical aspects of recording and sending television images.
- To develop an appreciation of the multiplicity of uses of television in today's world.
- To provide pupils an opportunity to read nonfiction.

OBJECTIVES

The objectives listed below refer to specific skills for which lessons are presented in the Reading and Language section for this story. Many other skills are developed in Word Highlights, Interpretation and Comprehension, and through annotations. After reading the selection and participating in the discussion and activities, pupils should be able to demonstrate the following abilities.

1. To describe the relationship between stress, usage, and meaning.

2. To match English words with their Latin sources, *pro-, re-, jacere,* and *flectere.*

3. To identify words that sound alike but are spelled differently.

4. To identify a given word as noun or adjective, depending upon its use in a sentence.

5. To demonstrate a method of taking notes using subheads and important details.

6. To distinguish between fact, opinion, and misinformation.

Teaching Strategies

WORD HIGHLIGHTS

1. The author of this essay talks about three important communications satellites. Tell your pupils the three names and have them try to figure the logic behind each one. The three are Early Bird (so named because it was the first of the commercial [i.e., private] communication satellites to be launched); Telstar (named by combining the form *tel(e)-* as in *television* or *telephone* and *star;*) and Echo (named because of the way it bounced signals off its surface to a point back on earth).

2. Read each of the following sentence pairs aloud and write the italicized word in each pair on the board. Have pupils indicate which sentence in a pair uses the italicized word in a new, modern meaning and which uses the word in an older, original meaning. Have pupils explain how the modern meaning differs from the original.

   a. A large art museum may have thousands of *pictures* in its collection.   Original.
   Motion *pictures* have developed into an art form of their own.   Modern.

   b. The *waves* along the beaches of Hawaii are excellent for surfing.   Original.
   The air is filled with *waves* — light waves, sound waves, and other kinds as well.   Modern.

   c. Some Americans think we should slow down our exploration of   Modern.
   outer *space*.
   Canada covers much *space* in North America.   Original.

   d. Airplane traffic can disrupt a television *signal*.   Modern.
   A train engineer relies on *signals* for his directions.   Original.

   e. Many sports events are *broadcast* live on radio and television.   Modern.
   One way to feed chickens is to *broadcast* seed over the ground.   Original.

   f. Nail polish covers nails with a thin, protective *film*.   Original.
   You ruin *film* if you expose it to bright sunlight.   Modern.

3. The combining form *tel-* or *tele-* comes from the Greek word *tele*, meaning *far, at a distance. Television* literally means *seen at a distance,* to describe the transmission of signals over long distances to produce a picture. Develop the use of *tele-* further with *telephone* (*tele-* plus Gk *phone,* sound), *telegraph* (*tele-* plus Gk *graphein,* to write), *telescope* (*tele-* plus Gk *skopein,* to view). Elicit more examples of *tele-* words. (Telepathy, teletype, telegram.)

4. Write on the board the following Glossary words; read them aloud with the pupils, and have each word used in a sentence.

cable (TV)	newscast	reflectors	transmission
commercial	orbit	rehearsed	transmitted
edited	orbital	relaying	taped
magnetic	projected	satellite	tube

   Have pupils master the pronunciation of the following Glossary words:

advantages	aquanauts	automatically	imparting	launched

INTRODUCING THE SELECTION

The first story in this unit treated television in a humorous way. The selection you are about to read takes a more serious look at the same subject. Who will read the title aloud? Can you predict from the title what in particular the article will be about? (No, the title is general enough to include the invention and development of television, its technical operation, and television production.)

The world of television has its own special vocabulary. In order to understand a technical article, such as "What Television Is," you have to know the meaning of the important words and concepts before you begin. Many "television" words are probably familiar to you already.

Write these words on the board:

network	panel show
cable	magnetic tape
telecast	on-the-scene
newscast	televised

Can you pick out words that describe particular types of programs? (Newscast, panel show.) Who can tell us what each kind of program is like? Who will find the phrase used when the television camera is present as the news is happening? (On-the-scene.) Which other words can you tell us about? Who will look up the others and give us their meanings?

Make sure the pupils understand each of the above words before they continue.

GUIDED SILENT READING

Each essay in this unit should be read in one sitting.

Because this selection is rich in technical information about television, it will be necessary for you to read slowly and carefully. You will find it helpful for understanding and remembering what you read if you write down in words and phrases the main ideas that you come across. You will have a chance to share them with each other after you have finished reading the selection silently.

Take a few minutes before Interpretation and Comprehension to hear pupils' notes.

What Television Is

JEANNE and ROBERT BENDICK

The word *television* means "to see far." What appears on your television screen started as a picture of something that could be seen, then

HUNDREDS WATCH SPACE LAUNCH ON TV IN GRAND CENTRAL STATION, NEW YORK CITY.

234

INTERPRETATION AND COMPREHENSION

SHARING PERSONAL EXPERIENCE

Can anyone tell us more than the text offers about the first steps in the process of televising a program? (Some pupils may be able to describe a television studio: the cameras, the monitors, cue cards, makeup. Choose a pupil to find out more about what happens in a TV studio and report back to the class.)

SKIMMING FOR IMPORTANT DETAILS

Who will read aloud the lines that describe the transmitting-receiving process? (Top of page 235.)

READING FOR THE MAIN IDEA

Read the first paragraph on page 235 silently. Which words do you think express the most important idea in the paragraph? ("Television is the greatest way ever invented of sending information across space.")

Have pupils discuss the ways in which television provides us with information.

what was seen became electricity, then radio waves, then electricity again—and finally a picture in your receiver, all in an instant.

But television is more than just a picture sent by radio waves and seen across space. Television is the greatest way ever invented of *sending information* across space. More people than ever before can now both see and hear the sights, sounds, and ideas of the world they live in.

Kinds of Television Programs

There are three kinds of programs for television: live, tape, and film. A program may be any one of these or a combination of all of them.

A live television program is the transmission of an event or action as it actually takes place at that moment. It might be a program from a television studio, such as a play or a panel show which has been planned and rehearsed. It might be an on-the-scene broadcast of a sports or a news event that is happening. A live program is televised with a television camera as it happens.

A taped show is taken with a television camera, too. Pictures are immediately recorded on magnetic tape for a later showing. A taped show can be edited, shortened, or changed in other ways. It can be corrected, and parts of it can be done over. A taped program can also be repeated. But a live show is seen just as it happens, and it can be seen "live" only once.

235

Punctuation Signals
"—and finally a picture." Dash contributes emphasis and aids readability.
"programs for television:" Colon signals elaboration fo follow.
"on-the-scene broadcast." Hyphens link elements of phrase used as adjectival modifier.
"live." Quotation marks prevent confusion of meaning.

information
From L *in-*, into, plus *formare*, to form, plus *-ation*, act of. Relate *reformation, transformation, formal, informal, transform, uniform, uniformity, formula.*

event
From L *eventus*, a happening, related to *venire*, to come. Relate *invent, adventure, misadventure, circumvent, prevent, avenue.*

What are the three kinds of television programs mentioned? (Live, tape, and film.) Now read the rest of this section silently.

What is meant by "live television"? What are some types of live programs mentioned? (Play, panel show, sports, or news event.) Which is rehearsed, a sports event or a play? Is there any word similar in meaning to *rehearse* that would describe the activity that takes place before athletes actually compete? (Practice or training.) In what ways does a taped broadcast differ from a live one? Find and read the lines that explain this. (Paragraph 4.) Which kind of show do you think would be more interesting to watch? Why? Can you think of any dangers involved in seeing only taped television programs? (Discuss with pupils the fact that tapes can be edited in such a way that they give a false impression of what really happened.)

READING FOR THE MAIN IDEAS

MAKING COMPARISONS

THINKING CRITICALLY

T•399

A filmed program is photographed on film with a motion-picture camera. Film can be used in more ways than tape. For regular television series, film is sometimes less expensive than tape. The finished film must be projected onto a special television tube in order to be transmitted.

All three kinds of television programs can be in black and white or in color.

Sometimes television cameras are used to pick up a play, and then the television pictures are photographed on motion-picture film from a special tube. This film can be shown later in theaters or on television.

Relaying the Signal

The waves which carry television signals cannot be broadcast over long distances as can those which carry an ordinary radio program. Ordinary radio waves take long, easy bounces around the earth. But television radio waves are very short. They stop as soon as they come to earth or go shooting off into space where the earth curves. For this reason, direct television broadcasts cannot usually be received more than sixty or seventy miles from where they start.

236

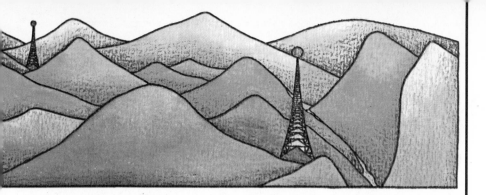

A network of relay stations and cables usually sends the signals over longer distances. Relay stations are placed on hills or mountains, as far apart as they can be and still be within line of sight of each other. On top of a relay station are big reflectors which scoop up the television signals aimed at them. Inside the relay station special equipment strengthens the signals and sends them out again, on to the next station. This equipment works automatically. There does not have to be anybody at the station at all.

Relay by Communications Satellites

Television signals are relayed over very great distances by communications satellites. There are several kinds of satellites. They orbit the earth at various heights. One kind orbits the earth from about 600 to 3,500 miles up. Telstar is this kind of satellite.

Another kind of satellite matches the earth's orbital speed and therefore keeps a fixed position, 22,300 miles up. Early Bird is an example of this kind of satellite.

237

automatically
From Greek (Gk) *auto-,* self, plus *matos,* thinking or willing, plus *-ically,* relating to. Relate *automation, automaton.*

satellite
From L *satelles,* attendant bodyguard of Roman kings. Meaning transferred to a man-made object that circles a heavenly body, such as the moon or the earth.

orbit
From L *orbis,* a circle. Hence, a circular path.

Early Bird
From aphorism: "The early bird gets the worm."

Who can explain in his own words how relay stations and cables make it possible for signals to travel over greater distances than direct television broadcasts? Who will read aloud the lines that describe the relay process to see if the explanation was right? (Paragraph 1.) Who will read the last subtitle aloud?

Use annotations to clarify meaning of *satellites* and *orbit.*

Now silently read all the material that has to do with communications satellites. A few of you will be asked to give a three-minute report on what you have read. Write down only the words and phrases you consider the key ones that will help you to remember the information you have read. If you see a word you don't know the meaning of, look it up.

Select a few pupils to give reports after clarifying the concepts of *orbiting, keeping a fixed position, reflective surface,* and *bounce-off place.*

GETTING THE MAIN IDEAS

SUMMARIZING INFORMATION

Echo was one of the first kinds of communications satellites. It was a large balloonlike satellite with a reflective surface. It did not contain any transmitter but was simply a bounce-off place for the signal between the sending and the receiving points. Echo I was launched in 1960 and burned out in 1968. It orbited the earth from about 640 to 800 miles up.

Television is still very young. The first practical television broadcasts were made around 1939. Commercial television started around 1947. In the years since then, television has become so much a part of our lives that it is hard to think of a time when it did not exist.

Not long ago it seemed a miracle to be able to see something across a city. Now we can see entertainment and watch events on other continents at the instant they are taking place. We can also learn about outer space by following the journeys of the astronauts. We can learn about inner space by following along with the aquanauts. Now people everywhere can enjoy the same things together and learn about each other and from each other. Television belongs to all the people in the world.

238

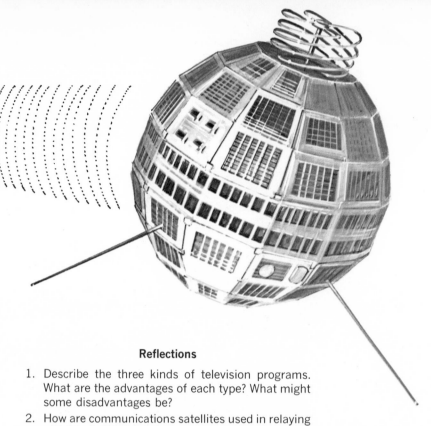

Reflections

1. Describe the three kinds of television programs. What are the advantages of each type? What might some disadvantages be?
2. How are communications satellites used in relaying television signals?
3. News stories that are televised live are often taped at the same time. Why might people who have seen only the taped broadcast of an event have a different idea of what had happened from people who saw the live broadcast? As a result, what should one keep in mind in viewing *taped* newscasts?
4. Some people think that television can do a better job of teaching (imparting information) than books can. Other people think the opposite is true. Which side of this argument would you take? Give reasons for your answer.

239

Suggest that pupils may want to read more about this subject in *Television Works Like This* by Jeanne and Robert Bendick.

Questions 1 and 2 provide a good review of the selection. Question 3 encourages critical thinking. Question 4 can be used as the basis of group discussion.

USING REFLECTIONS

READING AND LANGUAGE

I. READING SKILLS

OBJECTIVE 1

● **To describe the relationship between stress, usage, and meaning. (Phonology)**

Duplicate or write the following words and respellings on the board.

Words	Pronunciations	
	1	**2**
record	rek'ərd	ri kôrd'
relay	rē'lā	ri lā'
project	proj'ekt	prə jekt'
present	prez'ənt	pri zent'
conduct	kon'dukt	kən dukt'
permit	pėr'mit	pėr mit'
object	ob'jekt	əb jekt'
rebel	reb'l	ri bel'

Study the words and the alternate pronunciations for each. How are the pronunciations in column 1 alike? (Accent on first syllable.) in column 2? (Accent on last syllable.)

Can you tell which pronunciation to use just by looking at the words? (No.) What else do you need to help you decide? (Context—situational or sentence.) Who can think of a sentence using one pronunciation of any word? (Accept reasonable answers.)

Look at the first sentence on page 237. How is *r-e-l-a-y* pronounced? (re'la.) Why? (It is used as a noun.) Where is the primary accent? (On the first syllable.) Now look at the first sentence in the second paragraph on that page. Is the pronunciation the same? (No.) Why not? (Here *relay* is used as a verb.) Where is the primary accent? (On the second syllable.) If you didn't put the stress in the right place, would the meaning be as clear? (No.)

Now think about vowel sounds. When the primary accent shifts to a different syllable, might the vowel sounds change? (Yes.) Which word shows no vowel sound change? (Permit.)

Who can state a pronunciation rule for the words in the lesson? (When certain words are used as nouns, the primary stress is on the first syllable. When these words are used as verbs, the primary stress is on the second syllable. When primary stress shifts, vowel sounds may change.)

Duplicate or write on the board the following sentences.

T•404 Have pupils write the pronunciations of the under-

lined words in the sentences and label each pronunciation noun or verb.

1. A person who wants to rebel is called a rebel.

   ri bel'–verb; reb'l–noun

2. A learner's permit can permit driving.

   pėr'mit–noun; pėr mit'–verb

3. I object to that ugly object.

   əb jekt'–verb; ob'jekt–noun

4. His friend will present him with a present.

   pri zent'–verb; prez'ənt–noun

5. Listen as the musicians record songs for their record.

   ri kôrd'–verb; rek'ərd–noun

6. If your conduct is good, conduct the lesson!

   kon'dukt–noun; kon dukt'–verb

Have pupils use the following words as both nouns and verbs in written sentences. They may check their dictionaries for stress and meaning. *refuse, contest, digest, escort,* and *suspect.*

OBJECTIVE 2

● **To match English words with their Latin sources, pro-, re-, jacere, and flectere. (Morphology)**

Write the following sentences on the board and have them read.

The film was projected on the screen.

On top of relay stations are large reflectors.

Who will read the sentences aloud? Who can tell us the meanings of the underlined words from context clues? (*Projected* means *thrown forward; reflectors* means *devices that turn back heat, light, etc.*)

Explain that these words come from Latin sources. Write the following on the board and help pupils to see the relationship between the meanings of the English words and the meanings of the Latin roots and affixes.

projected   *pro-*, forth, plus *ject,* from *jacere,* to throw, plus *-ed.*

reflectors   *re-*, back, plus *flect,* from *flectere,* to turn, plus *-or,* an agent, plus *-s.*

Jacere and *flectere* are the Latin sources for the roots of many other English words. Knowledge of the meaning of their word parts will be a clue to the meaning of many words. Let's see if you can match some of these other English words with their Latin roots.

Present the following exercise to the class.

Read the words in the list. Then write them under the Latin words from which they come, and use the English words in sentences.

projection	flexible	deflect	dejected
reflex	inject	reject	inflection

jacere	**flectere**
projection	reflex
inject	flexible
reject	deflect
dejected	inflection

OBJECTIVE 3

● **To identify words that sound alike but are spelled differently. (Semantics)**

Pronounce the pairs of words below.

tea—tee	scene—seen	their—there
days—daze		principal—principle

Could you distinguish the words in each pair from their sounds? (No.)

Write the word pairs on the board.

Now can you tell the meanings of these sound-alikes?

Write the term *homophone* on the board.

Homo- means *one; phone* means *sound.* Homophones sound alike but are different in meaning and spelling. In what ways are the words on the board different? (Spelling and meaning.)

Have pupils use each word in an oral sentence to indicate its meaning.

OBJECTIVE 4

● **To identify a given word as noun or adjective, depending upon its use in a sentence. (Syntax)**

When you refer to a dictionary for the use of a word, is there ever more than one use given? (Yes.) How can you tell to what class a word belongs, for example whether it is a noun or an adjective? (You must see how it is used in a given sentence.)

Write the following two sentences on the board.

The word television means to "see far."

The television program was canceled.

How is *television* used in the first sentence, or what word class does it belong to? (Noun.) How do you know? (It names something that comes before a verb; it's marked by the determiner *the.*) How is *television* used in the second sentence? (As an adjective.) How do you know? (Its place in the sentence, before a noun, tells what kind of program.)

Have the pupils listen to the sentences below or put them on the board. If you read the sentences aloud repeat the underlined word.

Tell whether the underlined words are used as adjectives or as nouns.

1. Peter received a new radio.	noun
2. Radio waves are very short.	adjective
3. He moved with a smooth motion.	noun
4. Watching television is like watching a motion picture.	adjective

What other words can you suggest that may be used as a noun or an adjective?

Write pupils' suggestions on the board. Divide the class into pairs to choose a few words from the list. Have one student in each pair write sentences using the words as nouns and the other using them as adjectives. Have the pair exchange papers to check each other's work. Advise pupils that most common nouns in English may be used as adjectives.

OBJECTIVE 5

● **To demonstrate a method of taking notes using subheads and important details.**

Taking notes is useful in preparing reports, reviewing for tests, and generally in understanding what is read.

Write the following framework on the chalkboard.

Introduction: Description of Television
    I. Kinds of Television Programs
        Live, Tape, Film
    II. Relaying the Signal
        Reason for relaying television waves, and
        how it is done with cables and relay stations
    III. Relay for Communications Satellites

Summary: Expanding Opportunities in Entertainment, Education, and Science

T•405

Develop the idea that listing the subheads from the text is a technique for taking notes. Have pupils fill in the framework by adding the headings from the essay. They may then jot down a few important words or phrases under each heading, including important ideas found in the introductory and summary paragraphs.

II.   LITERARY SKILLS

OBJECTIVE 6

● **To distinguish between fact, opinion, and misinformation.**

Pupils should be encouraged to think critically about what they read. Help them to develop guidelines for distinguishing between fact, opinion, and misinformation.

What do "What Television Is" and "The Television-Chocolate Room" have in common? (Television is the central focus of each; each tells something about how television works.) What is the most important difference between the two selections? (One is a fictional story, with fictional characters, setting, and action; the other is a serious piece of nonfiction.)

Why do you suppose the Bendicks wrote this essay? (To give readers basic information about television, to express opinions about the subject, and to influence readers' attitudes about television.) Is the essay made up only of facts? (No, it is a mixture of fact and opinion.) Why does the reader have to use judgment when reading this, or any, essay? (He must be careful not to confuse fact with opinion or misstatement of facts.)

It is useful to know whether an author is qualified to write on a particular subject. As I read a short biographical statement about the Bendicks, the authors of this essay, you decide whether they are well qualified to be good authors for this essay. (After reading the biographical note on TE page 395, encourage pupils to give their reactions.) How could you check further to see whether the information given in the essay is reliable? (Volunteers may want to check the information with another source.)

Do the Bendicks differ from Roald Dahl in their attitude toward television? If so, how? (Yes, they seem to consider it a wonderful invention; Mr. Dahl seems to disapprove of it.) Skim pages 235 and 238 of the essay for evidence of the Bendicks' enthusiasm. (Page 235, paragraph 2; page 238, last paragraph.) What kinds of information could the Bendicks have included if they had wanted to present a more well-rounded picture of the advantages and disadvantages of television? (Accept all reasonable answers.)

The following may be presented orally or as a written exercise. Ask pupils to be ready to give reasons for their answers.

Decide whether you think each statement is one of Fact, Opinion, or Misinformation and write *F*, *O*, or *M* in the blank at the end of the statement.

1. Television is the greatest way of sending people across space.   M

2. Television broadcasts cannot usually be received more than sixty or seventy miles from where they start because television radio waves are very short.   F

3. Television may eventually put books out of existence.   O

4. Because the television audiences are large, commercial products can be presented to many people at once.   F

5. Bits of photographs suddenly hit a television antenna where a wire leads them into the back of the television set, and there they get fitted together, and the photograph appears on the screen.   M

6. A network of relay stations and cables usually sends the television signals over long distances.   F

7. A live television program is the transmission of an event or action as it actually takes place at that moment.   F

8. Now, thanks to television, people everywhere can enjoy the same things together and learn about each other and from each other.   O

9. The bigger the object to be photographed for television, the better.   M

10. Sometimes television cameras are used to pick up a play, and then the television pictures are photographed on motion-picture film.   F

III.   REGROUPING
FOR INDIVIDUAL NEEDS

Reinforcement Activities

The following reteaching activities are suggested for use with pupils who had difficulty with the Evaluation Masters. The teacher should develop additional exercises as needed.

Objective 3: List on the chalkboard and discuss the meaning of the following pairs of homophones. Have pupils use them orally in sentences.

pale	blue	pair	plain
pail	blew	pare	plane

For written practice, have the pupils find a homophone for the following words and use each one in a sentence: *beet* (beat), *piece* (peace), *right* (write), *see* (sea), *knew* (new).

Objective 4: In the following paired sentences, have pupils label the underlined word noun and adjective.

1. She drank milk from a glass. (Noun)

   The glass ornament on the Christmas tree broke when it fell. (Adjective)

2. The guest house is not used in winter. (Adjective)

   Mary was our guest this week end. (Noun)

3. Beth likes to play with paper dolls. (Adjective)

   The paper was thrown on the front porch. (Noun)

4. Sugar is sweet. (Noun)

   Mother baked some sugar cookies. (Adjective)

Objective 6: To help pupils separate fact from opinion, develop approximately ten sentences which are clearly either fact or opinion, for example:

1. I think Mary is a nice girl. (Opinion)
2. Spinach is delicious. (Opinion)
3. New York City is in the state of New York. (Fact)
4. Man has walked on the moon. (Fact)

Following discussion, encourage pupils to suggest other sentences which are either fact or opinion.

Extension Activities

Objective 3: Duplicate the following paragraph. Have pupils select a homophone for each underlined word and use it in a sentence.

I bought some postcards when we were in Washington, D.C. I sent several with pictures of monuments to friends, and one with a scene of the Cherry Blossom Festival to my principal.

Objective 6: Have pupils bring in newspaper articles, editorials, and magazine articles that contain examples of fact, opinion, and misinformation. Use for class discussion.

IV. ENRICHMENT

● One of the industries that has grown with the increase in television viewing is the national poll, or "ratings" system that tries to determine how many people are watching television and what percentage of the viewers are watching certain shows. Have pupils conduct their own version of a ratings poll by surveying the viewing habits of their parents, relatives, and friends.

● Try to arrange a trip to a local television station. Have pupils pay particular attention to such things as the control room, the studios and the electrical equipment, the scenery and sets. Discuss how complicated it must be to produce a television show. Lead pupils to understand that the high cost of putting on a television show is one reason that public, or noncommercial, television has been slow to realize its full potential.

● Develop a discussion of the uses of television, using the following questions as a guide: "Has television helped you better understand people in your culture or other cultures? How?" "In what ways might television help countries to get along?" Have students share their ideas by writing an essay entitled: "Television, an Aid to World Understanding."

One for the Univac (pages 240–251)

SUMMARY

According to Rupert Price's definition, a Univac is "an electric machine that can answer almost anything." Young Albert Einstein Smedley, a reputed scientific genius who was visiting in Wakefield, declared that it was impossible to make a Univac without using expensive laboratory facilities. But Rupert and his pals showed Albert they could build a Univac from an old piano crate, a carpet sweeper, an electric fan, and a dog clipper. They placed it on the front lawn of Rupert's home along with a sign offering to answer any question for five cents.

Rupert's mother was the first to ask a question of the Univac, and with a tremendous noise it ejected the answer through a slot. Several of the other mothers tried it. All of them found the answers appropriate and amusing. The Univac was one of the attractions at the Dad's Club Carnival the next evening. Albert's mother insisted that such a contraption was too childish to interest her son. Imagine her surprise to find that Albert was actually inside the Univac, pounding out answers on a typewriter!

ABOUT THE AUTHOR

A registered nurse living in Green Bay, Wisconsin, Ethelyn M. Parkinson is a full-time free-lance writer. Born in Oconto County, a member of the eighth generation of her family in the state, she attended Oconto Falls Normal School. Her books for children include *Good Old Archibald, Merry Mad Bachelors, Elf King Joe, Today I Am a Ham,* and *The Terrible Troubles of Rupert Piper,* from which this selection is taken.

MATERIALS

- Workbook pages 57–59.
- Evaluation Masters for "One for the Univac."

HUMAN VALUES

- To help children appreciate the inventiveness of a boy as opposed to a machine.
- To relate story characters' experience to pupil's own.
- To enjoy the humorous aspects of the story.

OBJECTIVES

The objectives listed below refer to specific skills for which lessons are presented in the Reading and Language section for this story. Many other skills are developed in Word Highlights, Interpretation and Comprehension, and through annotations. After reading the selection and participating in the discussion and activities, pupils should be able to demonstrate the following abilities.

1. To demonstrate stress in spoken and written language.
2. To demonstrate the use of noun suffixes *-ence, -ance, -ion, -tion,* and *-ation* by selecting the correct words for sentences.
3. To demonstrate the use of personal pronouns as noun substitutes.
4. To identify possessive pronouns.
5. To identify and describe onomatopoetic words.
6. To identify and describe story setting and scene changes in a given selection.
7. To describe important traits of story characters by matching descriptive phrases with character.

Teaching Strategies

WORD HIGHLIGHTS

1. The word *contraption* is a blend of three words: *contrivance*, a mechanical device; *trap*, a device by which something is caught; and *invention*, a product of imagination and creativity. The stress of *contraption* is "ingenuity," not necessarily "effectiveness." Have pupils tell what blend is based on each of the following word pairs:

   a. smoke and fog   smog
   b. breakfast and lunch   brunch
   c. motor and hotel   motel
   d. camp and jamboree   camporee
   e. chuckle and snort   chortle

2. Ask, "How do you think *hamburger, pop,* and *ice cream* were named?" Explain that these three words, all from the story, have very easy etymologies. *Hamburger* is named for Hamburg, a city in Germany, and is a shortened form of *hamburger steak.* In earlier days soda was sealed in a bottle with a cork, and the explosive sound from the cork being removed from the bottle is how we get the name *pop. Ice cream* gets its name from the way it is made: the ingredients are stirred to a creamy consistency while they are being frozen.

   Write the following words on the board and have pupils research and report on their etymologies.

Foods Named for Places		Foods Named for the Way They Are Made		Foods Named for People
sardines	cheddar	popcorn	spaghetti	McIntosh apple
bologna	parmesan	popover	doughnut	praline
cantaloupe	roquefort	turnover	pancake	eggs benedict
tangerine	Gruyère	banana split		sandwich

   Sources for these word histories include etymological dictionaries and encyclopedias.

3. The following Glossary words consist of a word plus noun- or adjective-forming suffixes:

   connection (connect + -ion)   **reference** (refer + -ence)
   marvelous (marvel + -ous)   **responsible** (response + -ible)
   prospector (prospect + -or)

   Write these words along with the base words and affixes on the board. Have pupils write two sentences for each word, one using the entire word and one, the word without the suffix.

4. Have pupils use each of the following words in a sentence:

Albert Einstein	carnival	horrible
amateur	clipper	legion
brilliant	engineer	shanty
	genius	

INTRODUCING THE SELECTION

Write the heading *Modern Scientific Inventions* on the board.

Television is one of the great inventions of our modern age. What other things come to your mind when you see this heading?

As pupils suggest them, list such inventions as radio, airplanes, submarines, electric light. Then add laser, transistor, computer, radar, vacuum tube.

Who knows which of the last five inventions is sometimes called an electronic brain? (Computer.) The word *computer* comes from the Latin *computare*, to count. A computer is an electronic machine that performs mathematical operations. Way back in about 600 B.C., the Chinese invented the first counting machine, the abacus, but that was operated manually. Can anyone describe an abacus to us?

Men learn ways of doing things quickly and efficiently.

Some of today's electronic computers can perform nearly a billion mathematical operations in one day!

You will read more about computers in the essay that follows the story you are about to read.

The transistor and the vacuum tube have made possible the computer and many other inventions. Who would like to find out more about vacuum tubes and transistors for us? Who will find out more about the laser?

The story you are going to read is about a computer that is put together by amateurs.

Write *amateurs* on the board. Have someone look up the word in the Glossary.

Have you ever been amateur inventors or builders? What did you make? Were you pleased with the results of your efforts? The boys in this story were probably even more successful than they had hoped to be.

GUIDED SILENT READING

Before pupils begin Interpretation and Comprehension, pose these questions: What is the best result to come from the boys' invention? Which of the adults in the story do you like best? Why?

Univac
Acronym: Universal automatic computer.

Albert Einstein (1879–1955)
Famous German-born American theoretical physicist, especially known for theory of relativity.

One for the Univac
ETHELYN M. PARKINSON

A Second Einstein

We might never have had a Univac if we had not met Albert Einstein Smedley. Albert came to visit in Wakefield during the teachers' meeting vacation.

I first heard about him at breakfast Thursday morning.

"Rupert," my mother said, "what in the world are you dreaming about?"

"Oh, not much," I said. "I was thinking about something that is in Miss Smithwick's alley."

"Oh, dear!" Mom said. "I might have known!"

"What's in the alley, Rupert?" Dad asked.

"Well," I said, "Miss Smithwick's good old piano box is in the alley."

Ma looked at Dad and shook her head. "Why *is* it?" she said. "We are as smart as Don and

240

INTERPRETATION AND COMPREHENSION

IDENTIFYING NARRATOR AND PLACE SETTING
Who narrates this story? (Rupert Piper.) Where does the story take place? (Wakefield.)

UNDERSTANDING A CHARACTER
As the story begins, what are Rupert's mother's first words to him? (Paragraph 3.) Why do you suppose she reacts as she does to Rupert's answer? What answer do you think she would prefer? (Perhaps she half-seriously would like Rupert to be a third Albert Einstein.)

USING PICTURE CLUES
Look at the picture. What can you tell from the expression on Rupert's face? (He is daydreaming.)

RELATING READING TO EXPERIENCE
Do you daydream? Are your daydreams ever about great and important things? (Give pupils an opportunity to share some of their fantasies.)

Irene Smedley. Why would their child be a second Einstein, while ours dreams great dreams about a piano box in an alley? *Why?*"

"That," Dad said, "is one for the Univac."

This was a very good answer. A Univac is an electric machine that can answer almost anything. You just feed the question into it, and it buzzes and whirs, and little lights blink, and after a while out pops the answer.

I ate my Pop-O's and drank my milk. "Excuse me," I said.

Mom said, "Where are you going?"

"Well, to find the guys."

"Naturally! And then where?"

"Ma," I said, "that's a toughie. That is one for the Univac."

Mom looked at Dad. "Now!" she said. "See what you started, Mr. Piper! Rupert, if you have any notion of bringing that piano box home, you get it right out of your head—while the Smedleys are in town. I won't have Mrs. Smedley saying that our son is a trash picker!"

I hated to tell the fellows. So I waited until afternoon when we were sitting out back of our garage, on the piano box.

"How did your mom know what we were going to do?" Milt said.

I said, "That's one for the Univac. Mothers are funny. It would take a brain machine to figure them out."

241

Why
Used three times in a paragraph as first word in a question. Emphasis added when it stands alone and is italicized.

"buzzes and whirs"
Imitative verbs.

Alliteration
"little lights blink"

Pop-O
Typical product name.

Slang
toughie. A difficult problem.

Who will find and read aloud the definition of a Univac? (Paragraph 2.) Why does Mr. Piper say, "That's one for the Univac"? (He implies that the question is too difficult for him to answer.)

INTERPRETING DIALOGUE

When Rupert uses the same expression, his mother seems to be annoyed with Rupert's father. How does her manner of addressing him indicate this? (Her formality suggests distance and cool feelings.) Why is this expression annoying to hear? (It is an evasive tactic.)

UNDERSTANDING A CHARACTER

How do you suppose Mrs. Piper guesses what is on Rupert's mind anyway? Does your mother ever read your mind in this way?

RELATING READING TO EXPERIENCE

Who will find the lines that show whether or not Rupert took Mrs. Piper's warning seriously? (Paragraph 9.) Although he seems not to have, is there any evidence to suggest that Rupert does respect her ability to read his mind? (Last paragraph.)

MAKING INFERENCES

"amateur master plumber"
"Master" of a trade is qualified to work independently and train apprentices. (Term was used in medieval guilds.) Here it sets up a contradiction with "amateur," one lacking professional qualification, who pursues an activity for enjoyment.

"Oh-oh!"
Ejaculation that often suggests suspicion as well as surprise.

porch
From L *porticus,* covered passage supported by columns. The word is related to *port,* a harbor or a gate. Relate *portico, porter, portal.*

"Well," Clayte said, "we will not take up any of her yard. All her troubles will be over as soon as we get this good old piano box up in this tree."

"Right!" Dood said. "But how are we going to do it?"

Just then a car came down our drive. It was Opal's father, Mr. Duncan. "Hello, gentlemen!" he said. "Rupert, your dad said he'd leave some plumbing tools in the garage where a good amateur master plumber could borrow them. Hey! What's this?" He looked at the piano box. Next he looked up in the tree and smiled a very big smile. "A very good idea!" he said. "If you'll wait until tomorrow, I'll help you put it up there."

He got the tools and drove away.

"How did he know?" Milt said.

"Well," I said, "he is an electrical engineer. Maybe he has a Univac."

Right then Mom called me. "Rupert? Rupert Piper! Come here!"

"Oh-oh!" Clayte said. "I just knew this would happen!"

But Mom was not mad. She was standing on the back porch with my basketball in her hands, and Annabelle and Albert were with her. Their mothers had come to call.

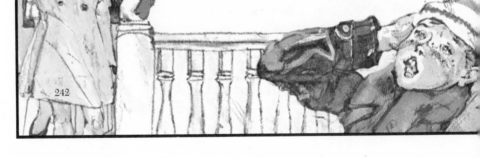

242

USING IMAGINATION — How do you suppose the boys plan to use the piano box once they get it into the tree? (Answers will vary.) Mr. Duncan appears just in time to help. Who will read the paragraph of his dialogue aloud? (Paragraph 3.)

APPRECIATING HUMOR — Once they understand the meanings of *amateur* and *master plumber*, pupils should detect the humor in Mr. Duncan's use of such contradictory terms in reference to himself.

IDENTIFYING WITH CHARACTERS — What is it about Mrs. Piper's summons to Rupert that suggests she may be angry? (Her insistent tone and her formality.) How do you suppose the boys feel when they discover that she is not? (Relieved.)

"Now you can have a lot of fun throwing baskets," Mom said.

"Mom," I said, "it's cold."

"It's a nice, mild February day," Mom said. "You've been outside all day, and you can enjoy it a bit longer."

"Well," Dood said, "I think I will be going."

"Me, too," said Milt and Clayte.

Mom smiled very sweetly. "Your mothers are dropping in, boys. They expect to find you here playing with Albert and Annabelle." She shut the door.

Albert was taking a little stroll in the yard, looking at things.

Annabelle said, "Albert simply has to get away by himself, to dream great dreams. His mother says so. She wishes he would share his great thoughts with mankind. But she says someday the world will know, when Albert has his private little chain of satellites around the sun."

Well, we did not want a little chain of satellites around the sun. All we wanted was a house in a tree.

Albert came back, looking excited. "Rupert," he said, "what is that big box doing back of your garage?"

243

"to get away by himself, to dream great dreams"
Parodies popular idea of the theoretical scientist or philosopher as highly impractical.

mankind
The human race. Suffix -*kind* implies association by nature, by birth.

If Mrs. Piper didn't get her way with Rupert earlier, she succeeds this time in getting Rupert, Dood, Clayte, and Milt to do just what she wishes. How? (In paragraphs 3 and 6 she exerts subtle but persuasive pressure. Have pupils discuss their understanding of the power behind her unspoken words.)

UNDERSTANDING CAUSE AND EFFECT

According to Annabelle, what kind of a boy is Albert? (A genius.) From whom did she get this impression? (Mrs. Smedley.) Mrs. Smedley wishes Albert could share his great dreams with everyone. Which word means *everyone*? (Mankind; see annotation.)

INTERPRETING DIALOGUE; RECOGNIZING SYNONYMS

To share something with mankind is certainly generous. Does anything that Annabelle says about Albert's mother suggest that perhaps her dreams for Albert aren't quite so noble? (Mrs. Smedley's dream of Albert's having his private chain of satellites around the sun carries with it the ring of self-interest.)

RECOGNIZING MOTIVATION

Punctuation Signal
"—or your money back." Dash indicates pause before final important phrase. Typical device in advertising messages.

Overstatement
"My teeth almost dropped out."

Typographical Clue
that. Italics for emphasis.

"Well," I said, "I suppose that is one for the Univac."

"Univac?" Albert said. "You can't make a Univac out of a piano box!"

Milt poked me. "Oh, indeed you can!" Milt said. "You can, Albert, if you know enough science. And we do!" Milt put his hands in his pockets and kind of rocked on his heels and smacked. He said, "Our Univac will be just about the best Univac in the U.S.A. It will answer all questions correctly within five minutes—or your money back."

My teeth almost dropped out. So did Dood's and Clayte's. We weren't *that* sure about making the Univac.

Albert's face was very red. He said, "I have a fine laboratory at home. It cost hundreds of dollars! But I cannot make a Univac."

"You do not need a laboratory to build a Univac," Milt said. "You just need to know how!" he smacked. "And we do!"

So the next morning we were working very hard in my backyard when Annabelle came along with Sylvia and Opal and Albert.

The girls stopped to ask a few very personal questions. "What in the world are you boys doing with that old sweeper and that old beat-up fan and that old dog clipper?" Opal said through her nose.

"Or is it a secret?" Sylvia said.

244

INTERPRETING DIALOGUE

What does Rupert's reply to Albert mean? (Rupert is putting Albert off.) Why do you think Rupert doesn't tell Albert immediately what he and his friends are planning to do? (Perhaps the boys expect Albert to be arrogant.)

Does Albert realize that Rupert is stalling him with his answer? (No, he takes his answer literally.)

RECOGNIZING PLOT DEVELOPMENT

How does Milt contradict Albert? Who will read Milt's lines? (Paragraph 3.) Do you suppose Milt had the idea of building a Univac before that moment? (Paragraph 4 indicates that he and the other boys had thought about it.) How does Milt's speech affect the rest of the story? (The boys proceed to build a Univac.)

"Oh, no," I said. "We are willing to share our great thoughts with mankind. However, most of you happen to be girls, which is different."

Annabelle flipped her eyelashes at me. "Come on, Albert," she said.

But Albert stood still. "Excuse me," he said. "I think I shall stay here and learn how to build a Univac."

Univac, Inc.

So we worked on the Univac all day. Mr. Duncan helped us.

"I do not want all the boys in town to get fatal electric shocks and die," Mr. Duncan said. "I have a daughter to marry off someday."

He meant Opal. I peeked at Milt under my eyelids. Clayte and Dood and Albert were peeking at us, too. Dood began to whistle.

Mr. Duncan is very crazy about Opal, and we did not want to hurt his feelings and tell him that we do not plan to marry her.

He fixed all the Christmas tree lights in the Univac. He worked on the old sweeper, the fan, and the old dog clipper. Then he tested all the cords and connections so that no one would get a shock.

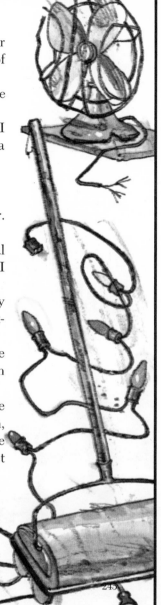

"most of you happen to be girls"
Note play on *mankind*. It is used here in a more limited sense than that in which it is generally used.

Univac, Inc.
Inc. is an abbreviation for incorporated (formed into a legal corporation for purposes of conducting business).

fatal
From L *fatalis*, deadly. Relate *fateful*, *fate*, *fatality*, *fatalism*.

"Christmas tree lights"
Appropriately used—in fact, flashing colored lights on an indicator panel are often referred to as "a Christmas tree."

Who will read Rupert's reply to the girls aloud? (Paragraph 1.) In what way is his answer humorous? (He makes a distinction between mankind and girls.)

Turn back a page. Read Opal's words to yourselves. Could she have expressed her curiosity in a way that would have produced a nicer response? When Rupert says that he and his friends have no intention of marrying Opal, what do you think he's really saying? (That he and his friends think of her as a pest.)

APPRECIATING HUMOR

UNDERSTANDING RELATIONSHIPS AMONG CHARACTERS

Slang
"very keen." Multiple meanings: bright, smart, wonderful, sharp. Compare paragraph 2, page 249.

Assonance and Rhyme
"keen green." Assonance is the repetition of sounds in words or syllables.

"prospector's hut . . . ice fisherman's shanty"
Both are temporary shelters, rudely and hastily built.

Punctuation Signal
ma'am. Contraction. Apostrophe marks omission of *d.*

We painted the Univac a very keen green color. Then we moved it onto our front lawn.

After a while Mom walked home from her club meeting with Albert's mother and all the other mothers, and you should have heard Mom scream.

"What is this horrible thing on my lawn? It looks like a prospector's hut or an ice fisherman's shanty!"

"No, ma'am," I said. "Please read the sign, ma'am."

NOTING STEPS IN A PROCESS

Skim page 245 and this one. Who will tell us what steps are mentioned as having gone into the preparation of the Univac? (Page 245, last paragraph; this page, first paragraph.)

FILLING IN LOGICAL STEPS

Having read the story silently before, you should be able to fill in certain details that are omitted at this point. What are they? Where might they be included? (Before the second paragraph; pupils must assume that the boys discussed their scheme: putting someone inside the machine, covering up the sound of his typing with all the other gadgets winking, blinking, whirring, and whining.)

CREATING NARRATION AND DIALOGUE

Have the pupils make up lines of dialogue and narration to create a bridge from the first to the second paragraphs on this page.

USING PICTURE CLUES

Look at the picture on this page. Who will tell us what the sign in the picture says? Is the Univac a streamlined machine? (No, it has all kinds of wires and gadgets on it.)

"I give up!" Mom said. "What did I ever do to deserve this?"

"Do you wish to ask the Univac?" I said. "Write it on this piece of paper and slip it in here, with a nickel."

So Mom put her question in the Univac. All the little lights began to wink and blink. The sweeper motor ran. The fan whirred. The dog clipper whined. Everything made a terrible noise. After a while the noise slowed down, and another slot opened, and out came the answer.

The answer was: "Don't worry, Mrs. Piper. This will make a lot of money."

Mom laughed. "Well, well! That's different! Do any of you ladies care to try the Univac?"

"It's amusing," Mrs. Smedley said. "However, Albert would be bored with any toy as childish as this."

Mom's cheeks got kind of pink. So did the other mothers'.

"I'll ask it something," Clayte's mother said, quite loud. So she found a nickel and wrote, "What can I fix quick for supper?"

The lights blinked, and the machines all roared, and the answer came out: "Bake some frozen chicken pies. Clayte can eat two."

"An excellent idea!" Mrs. Snow said.

Dood's mother said, "I'll ask it something, to see if it's honest." So she wrote a note: "Who is the smartest boy I know?"

247

"I give up!" .... "What did I ever do to deserve this?"
Ironic clichés.

nickel
Shortened from Swedish *kopparnickel*, niccolite ore.

Alliteration
"All the little lights .... whirred .... whined."

Assonance and Rhyme
"wink and blink"

The Univac responds to the questions with noise and activity. Who will find the verbs that express this? (Wink, blink, ran, whirred, whined, and roared.)

FINDING KEY VERBS

What impression do you get of Mrs. Piper from her reaction to the Univac's first answer? (Pupils will probably appreciate her light touch and sense of fun.) Who will read Mrs. Smedley's response, just as she probably speaks it? (Paragraph 6.) What does it tell you about her? (She is stuffy and not very understanding of the kinds of things boys enjoy.)

COMPARING CHARACTERS

Who will read the lines that tell how the other mothers react to Mrs. Smedley's comment? (Next paragraph: They are either angry or embarrassed.) How would you explain their reactions? (Answers will vary.)

The Univac almost shook to pieces, and then the answer came: "He is the boy who likes you best."

"How sweet!" Mrs. Hall said. "Thank you so much!" She patted the Univac.

Mrs. Willman dug a nickel out of her purse. She wrote: "Is Annabelle going to do the dishes tonight?"

This was a toughie. But the answer was good. Very good. "The prettiest and smartest girl at your house is going to do the dishes. Tell this to Annabelle."

"I'll try it, Univac," Mrs. Willman said. "If it doesn't work, I might try something else." She slapped her hands together and then laughed.

The Dad's Club carnival was the next night in Legion Hall. Mr. Duncan came around to my house at four o'clock.

"Rupert," he said, "how about moving the Univac down to the carnival? We can pick up some extra cash."

Whoever is in the Univac is being kept busy. Who will read Mrs. Hall's question and then explain how the Univac's answer reflects careful thought? (The answer avoids hurting anyone's feelings while at the same time flattering Mrs. Hall.) How might the question be answered less cleverly? as cleverly?

Who will read Mrs. Willman's question and the Univac's answer? (Paragraphs 3 and 4.) Do you think the Univac's answer is a good one? Why?

About how much time passes from the moment of the scene between the mothers and the Univac and Mr. Duncan's arrival at Rupert's house? (About a day.)

The cash was for our camp fund.

"A very keen idea," I said.

"Bring your crew of great scientists," Mr. Duncan said. "They will get some free ice cream and pop."

Well, the Univac was so busy that our crew of great scientists had to take turns working and eating.

After a while Mrs. Smedley came along. "Where on earth is Albert?" she said. "I haven't seen that boy since I got here!"

Right then Mr. Duncan came up, smiling. "Hello there, Mrs. Smedley," he said. "What do you think of the Univac?"

"It's very silly," she said.

Mr. Duncan laughed. "Come, now. It's a lot of fun. You ask Albert."

Mrs. Smedley kind of sniffed. "Albert wouldn't be interested in it. He's going to be a brilliant scientist."

"Well!" Mr. Duncan said. "What has he made?"

"Why, nothing—yet. He's learning."

"Then," Mr. Duncan said, "you'll be proud to know he helped make this Univac."

"I don't believe it!" Mrs. Smedley said.

Mr. Duncan winked at me. "Rupert," he said, "I'll risk a nickel on Albert. Ask the Univac where he is."

So I wrote: "Where is Albert?"

249

Overstatement
"crew of great scientists"

pop
Carbonated beverage gets its nickname from sound of cork popping when bottle is opened.

Idiom
"take turns." To take part in order, one after another.

Colloquialism
"Where on earth . . .?"

Who will read the words of Mr. Duncan's that reflect a friendly, teasing attitude toward the boys? (Paragraph 3.) How can you tell that Rupert enjoys Mr. Duncan's joke? (Next paragraph.)

INTERPRETING CHARACTERS THROUGH LANGUAGE

Read this page and the next silently. Who can tell us in his own words how Mrs. Smedley changes her attitude toward Albert and what part Mr. Duncan plays in the change? (Answers should show pupils' understanding of Mrs. Smedley's realization that her son is a normal boy with a normal need for fun and friends; Mr. Duncan points out how much fun Albert is having.)

UNDERSTANDING CHANGE IN A CHARACTER

Alliteration
"shivered and shook"

Colloquialism
"He sure is!"

Slang
"having himself a ball." Having fun.

"a very scientific secret"
A play upon "top secret" research projects for defense, space exploration, or commercial competition. Compare last paragraph, page 244.

Punctuation Signal
"if you want to break his heart—"
Dash indicates a significant pause that adds dramatic effect.

hamburger
American (Am) for Hamburger steak, ground meat patty, supposedly originated in the port city of Hamburg, Germany. Compare *frankfurter*.

The poor old Univac almost blew a fuse. It shivered and shook, and after a while the answer came: "I am very busy. Don't worry about me!"

Mrs. Smedley screamed. "Is my Albert in that contraption?"

"He sure is!" Mr. Duncan said. "My old typewriter is in there, and Albert is writing up these answers and having himself a ball. Of course, it's all a very scientific secret."

"That's right, Mrs. Smedley," I said. "Next it's Albert's turn to run the sweeper and the fan."

"And if you want to break his heart—you stop him!" Mr. Duncan said.

Mrs. Smedley stood and watched the Univac a long time. It was very busy.

At last Mrs. Smedley said, "Rupert, please give me a piece of paper." She wrote a question. "Would the Univac like a hamburger?"

The Univac shook, and the lights blinked. The answer came: "The Univac would like five hamburgers."

The hamburgers were very good, and Mrs. Smedley did not have to ask the good old Univac how many bottles of pop to order.

250

APPRECIATING HUMOR	Mr. Duncan says, ". . . it's all a very scientific secret" when he tells Mrs. Smedley about Albert and the typewriter. What does he mean? (He is being humorous: the boys have been pretending that the Univac worked electronically, but the brain behind it is a human one.)
DISCUSSING PERSONAL REACTIONS	Aside from the fact that Albert helped the boys make the Univac, can you think of other reasons why he would probably become part of their group now? (Through his cooperation and thoughtfulness, he shows the group that he is a very likable boy; the inflated image of him was his mother's, not his own. Also when his mother asks if he wants a hamburger, he orders one for each of the boys.)
DRAMATIZING DIALOGUE	Assign parts and have pupils dramatize the last two pages.

Reflections

1. Why do you think the Smedleys named their son Albert Einstein Smedley? Who was the "first" Albert Einstein? (If you don't know, look him up in an encyclopedia.)

2. At first, what did Rupert and his friends intend to do with the piano box? What did they end up doing with it?

3. The boys used each of the following things in their invention. What do you think was the purpose of each item?
   a. Christmas lights   d. An old dog clipper
   b. A sweeper motor   e. An old typewriter
   c. An old electric fan

4. When Albert asked for five hamburgers, what do you think he did with them? What does this show about him?

5. Choose the best ending for each of the sentences below, and explain your choice.
   a. To judge from this story, Albert Einstein Smedley
      • really was a genius.
      • was about as bright as the other boys.
      • was stupid.
   b. Annabelle probably did do the dishes that night because
      • she was a very responsible girl and enjoyed helping her mother.
      • she liked doing dishes.
      • she wouldn't want anyone else to be considered the prettiest and smartest girl in the house.

6. How does Rupert first describe a Univac? How would you describe a Univac? Compare your description and Rupert's with one in a reference book.

251

Suggest that pupils may want to read more about Rupert Piper in *The Terrible Troubles of Rupert Piper* by Ethelyn M. Parkinson.

Questions 1 and 6 provide good research topics. Questions 2, 3, and 4 can be used for review of the story. Question 5 gives exercises in drawing conclusions.

USING REFLECTIONS

READING AND LANGUAGE

I. READING SKILLS

OBJECTIVE 1

- **To demonstrate stress in spoken and written language. (Phonology)**

Skim page 244 and find the third sentence in the fourth paragraph. Who will read it aloud? ("We weren't *that* sure about making the Univac.") Which word has the greatest stress? *(That.)* How do you know? (It is in italics.) Why is it emphasized? (Rupert thought Milt's statement was exaggerated.) How else besides italics could you show emphasis if you were writing? (By underlining or using capital letters.) Where else in the story are italics used for stress? (Page 240, last line; page 241, third line.)

Write the following sentence on the board.

John stayed after school to help the committee.

Now listen to the questions I ask. Each question calls for a different way of reading the sentence. As I ask the question, look at the sentence on the board. Then write the word or words that you would stress in reading the sentence. Be ready to read the sentence that way.

1. Who stayed after school to help the committee?
(John.)

2. Why did John stay after school?
(To help the committee.)

3. What did John do to help the committee?
(Stayed after school.)

Spoken English has a stress-time rhythm. (Write *stress-time* on the board.) This means that when we speak, we stress certain words or syllables. In many sentences we say or read aloud, one syllable in the sentence receives primary stress. Much depends on meaning and what we feel is important in the sentence.

Write the following sentence on the board.

Rúpert made a Únivac.

Who will read the sentence aloud? Where did you hear stress? (On the syllables *Ru* and *U*.) Who will mark them with an accent? Which words are unstressed? (Made, a.) Words have primary stress if they are said alone; however, many words lose their stress in sentences because we rush to get to the stressed, or important, words. Also, something else happens; the unstressed words have

T·424 changes in their consonant and vowel sounds.

Write the following sentences on the board.

1. You might have knówn.
2. I ´am going to find them.
3. Hów did your móm know?
4. Will you sée him?
5. Héy, get your íces.

Look at the first sentence as I read it, and decide which words receive primary stress. Place an accent over these words. How might the sentence be rewritten to show the change in the unstressed words? (Y' might've known.)

Continue in the same way with remaining sentences.

OBJECTIVE 2

- **To demonstrate the use of noun suffixes -ence, -ance, -ion, -tion, and -ation by selecting the correct words for sentences. (Morphology)**

Write the following sentences on the board.

The connection of our electricity took three days.

Reference to a map will show you where that place is located.

Who will write on the board the base word and suffix for the underlined word in the first sentence? (Connect + -ion.) What does the suffix *-ion* mean in *connection* in this sentence? (Act of.) What does connection mean in this sentence? (Act of connecting.) The suffixes *-tion* and *-ation* are variant spellings of *-ion* and mean the same thing.

Who will write on the board the base word and suffix for the underlined word in the second sentence? (Refer + -ence.) What does the suffix *-ence* mean in *reference* in this sentence? (Act of.) What does *reference* mean in this sentence? (Act of referring.) The suffix *-ance* is a variant spelling of *-ence* and means the same thing as *-ence*. The addition of these suffixes changes verbs to nouns.

Duplicate and distribute the following exercises.

A. In the blank, write the base word for each of the following words, making the necessary spelling changes.

1. inference	infer	5. residence	reside
2. inspection	inspect	6. reflection	reflect
3. persistence	persist	7. creation	create
4. taxation	tax	8. guidance	guide

B. Read the words and sentences below. Then find a word in the list that will complete each sentence. Write the word in the blank. Use each word only once.

organization   appearance   attention
inventions   subtraction   preference

1. The photograph showed the change in her
   appearance .

2. She showed a   preference   for blue dresses.

3. In arithmetic, some pupils have trouble with
   subtraction .

4. He works for a large   organization .

5. Many   inventions   make life easier for people.

6. My pet will do almost anything to get
   attention .

OBJECTIVE 3

● **To demonstrate the use of personal pronouns as noun substitutes. (Syntax)**

Write the following words on the chalkboard.

I	he	we	me
you	they	she	them

These words are personal pronouns. What is a personal pronoun? (A word that takes the place of a person's name or title in a sentence.) Who can tell us why pronouns are used? (To avoid repetition.)

Indicate that pronouns and nouns are so closely related that they may often replace each other in a sentence. A pronoun is generally a clue to noun meaning because it is used instead of a noun. Write these sentences on the board and have them read. Ask pupils to cross out the second use of a noun or nouns and write a pronoun in its place.

           he
1. Albert came to visit Wakefield, and ~~Albert~~ made friends there.
2. Clayte and Dood and Albert came over because
           they
   ~~Clayte and Dood and Albert~~ wanted to work on the Univac.
              she
3. Mr. Duncan has a daughter; ~~the daughter~~ is named Opal.

Have pupils turn to page 245 in the story and list all the personal pronouns they can find, and tell to whom they refer. (I, we, our, you, we, he, she, us, my, his, him, her.)

OBJECTIVE 4

● **To identify possessive pronouns.**

Write these nouns on the board: *teachers, Miss Smithwick, prospector, iceman, Albert, children.* Then write the sentences that follow.

1. Albert came to visit in Wakefield during the teachers' vacation.

2. Miss Smithwick's good old piano box is in the alley.

3. Could that be a prospector's hut or an iceman's shanty?

4. Next, it is Albert's turn to work the sweeper and the fan.

5. That's the children's pool.

How did the underlined nouns change appearance in these sentences? (Addition of apostrophe to *teachers;* addition of *'s* to the other nouns.)

In the first sentence, did Albert or the teachers have a vacation? (The teachers.) What belonged to Miss Smithwick? (Piano box.) What might belong to a prospector? (A hut.) To an iceman? (A shanty.) What belonged to the children? (A pool.) What does the addition of an apostrophe or an *'s* show at the end of a noun? (Possession.)

Write on the board *mine, my, your, yours, his, her, hers, its, their,* and *theirs.* Identify them as possessive pronouns, or noun substitutes that stand for nouns that show possession.

Have pupils copy the sentences, cross out the underlined nouns and their markers, and substitute the correct pronouns from the list above.

1. Albert came to visit in Wakefield during
         their
   ~~the teachers'~~ vacation.

         Her
2. ~~Miss Smithwick's~~ good old piano box is in the alley.

              his
3. Could that be ~~the prospector's~~ hut?

          his
4. Next, it's ~~Albert's~~ turn to work the sweeper and the fan.

          their
5. That's ~~the children's~~ pool.

The possessive pronouns *my, your, her,* and *their* almost always come before a noun, the same as an adjective. The possessive pronouns *mine, yours, hers,* and *theirs* generally follow a verb, as in "That pool is *theirs.*" *His* and *its* can be used in either position.

● **To identify and describe onomatopoetic words. (Semantics)**

Write this quotation from the story on the board.

> You just feed the question into it, and it <u>buzzes</u> and <u>whirs</u>, and little lights blink, and after a while out <u>pops</u> the answer.

Who will underline the words that help us hear the Univac? Think for a minute how the Univac might have sounded as the author described it in the story. Name some things that buzz. (Saws, bees, etc.) Is a whir a soft or loud sound? (Soft.) What whirring sounds have you heard? (Small motors, fans, insect wings, etc.)

The word *pops* suggests that the answer came fast from the Univac. It might also suggest the sound the Univac made as it ejected an answer. What can you think of that makes a popping sound? (A bottle of soda being opened, bubble gum, etc.)

Write these words on the board: *whisper, fizz, hiss.*

Who will whisper the words I've written? Name something that fizzes and something that hisses. There is something alike about the words *buzz, whir, pop, whisper, fizz,* and *hiss.* What do you suppose the likeness is? (Pupils should realize that these words imitate sounds.)

Read the following sentences aloud and have pupils identify a word in each that imitates a sound.

1. The lights blinked, and the machine roared. (Roared.)
2. The sweeper blinked, and the dog clipper whined. (Whined.)
3. The dishes clattered in the kitchen. (Clattered.)
4. You can hear the squirrels chatter in the trees. (Chatter.)
5. We scraped the paint off the old table. (Scraped.)
6. The door closed with a click. (Click.)
7. The audience clapped to show its enjoyment. (Clapped.)

Some of the most commonly used imitative words are those we use to name animal sounds. Ask pupils to suggest some. (Bow-wow, mew, baa, etc.)

II. LITERARY SKILLS

● **To identify and describe story setting and scene changes in a given selection.**

What is the location of the story "One for the Univac"? (A place named Wakefield.) Does the author tell you which state Wakefield is in? (No, it could be anywhere in the United States.) Do you think the story is more or less interesting because Wakefield isn't set in a particular state? (Accept all answers, but point out that a vague setting gives each reader an opportunity to put his imagination to work.)

Would you say the story is set in a city, a suburb, or in the country? (Suburb.) How can you tell? (There are private houses close enough together for friends to visit, as well as back and front yards.) Is the specific setting of the story the same throughout? (No. Have pupils try to recall as many shifts of scene as they can.)

Have pupils take a few minutes to go through the story carefully and write down 1) the specific setting where a scene takes place, and 2) the page and line that reveal a scene is changing or has changed. The answers are as follows.

1. Rupert's kitchen

2. Rupert's kitchen to back of garage: "So I waited until afternoon when we were sitting out back of our garage, on the piano box." (P. 241, paragraph 9, second sentence.)

3. Behind Rupert's garage to back porch: "She was standing on the porch with my basketball in her hands, and Annabelle and Albert were with her." (P. 242, last paragraph.)

4. Rupert's back porch to backyard: "So the next morning we were working very hard in my backyard when Annabelle came along with Sylvia and Opal and Albert." (P. 244, paragraph 7.)

5. Rupert's backyard to front lawn: "Then we moved it onto our front lawn." (P. 246, second line.)

6. Rupert's front lawn to the Legion Hall: "Well, the Univac was so busy that our crew of great scientists had to take turns working and eating." (P. 248, last two paragraphs, and p. 249, paragraph 4.)

Choose one scene and draw a sketch of it. Make sure that your sketch is detailed enough so it could serve as the guide for a stage set if the story were to be rewritten into a play for presentation on the stage. Those who prefer could make a cardboard model of the scene.

OBJECTIVE 7

● **To describe important traits of story characters by matching descriptive phrases with character.**

After a discussion of the story characters, the following exercise may be duplicated and presented for independent work. Have pupils give reasons for their answers.

Below are the names of some of the characters in "One for the Univac" and various facts that apply to one or more of these characters. Look over the names and facts carefully and write in the blank next to each character's name the letter or letters of the phrases that apply. Then, on the next line, explain in more detail how one of these facts applies to the character.

1. Albert Einstein Smedley   a, h, i

   (Explanations will vary.)

2. Rupert Piper   a, b, d, h, k

3. Mrs. Piper   g, j

4. Mrs. Smedley   a, c, g

5. Mr. Duncan   b, f, h, k

    a. learns an important lesson
    b. teases
    c. is selfish
    d. fibs
    e. is considerate
    f. is handy
    g. cares about what people think
    h. is clever
    i. tries to live up to someone else's expectations
    j. pretends to be angry
    k. helps teach an important lesson

III. REGROUPING FOR INDIVIDUAL NEEDS

Reinforcement Activities

The following reteaching activities are suggested for use with pupils who had difficulty with the Evaluation Masters. The teacher should develop additional exercises as needed.

Objective 2: Duplicate the following chart for use as a work sheet.

Suffixes Meaning "the act of"

ion	tion	ation	ance	ence
connect	reduce	adore	appear	refer
connection	reduction	adoration	appearance	reference

Provide a model word for each suffix. Discuss the root words and elicit the change in word class from verb to noun once the suffix is added. Have pupils suggest other words for each column, using the text, Glossary, or dictionary.

Objective 6: Discuss with the pupils scene changes in a favorite television program when the action shifts. (Use any program viewed regularly by the pupils.) The pupils may list the scene changes that usually occur in one program and compare their answers.

Objective 7: Have pupils select one character from "One for the Univac" and skim the story to find descriptive phrases that indicate his character. They may compile a list of descriptive phrases, and then discuss the character as described in their list.

Extension Activities

Objective 5: The author's use of onomatopoetic words helps the reader imagine what the Univac was like. Have pupils write a paragraph describing something in terms of the sound it makes. They might tell about something mechanical, such as a motorcycle or power lawn mower, or something living—a child, puppy, or bird. Then they should underline the words they used that imitate sounds.   **T•427**

IV. ENRICHMENT

● Discuss the following quotations from the story to help pupils become more sensitive to character and feelings.

The following sentences from the story give clues to feelings. How observant are you? Can you discover how people are feeling and what they're like by studying what they do or say?

1. What does this passage (from pages 25–26) tell you about Rupert's parents? "We are as smart as Don and Irene Smedley. Why would their child be a second Einstein, while ours dreams great dreams about a piano box in an alley? Why?" (They might have resented Albert's arrival in Wakefield and be disappointed in Rupert.)

2. What do these sentences (from page 30) tell you about Milt? "Milt put his hands in his pockets and kind of rocked on his heels and smacked. He said, "Our Univac will be just about the best Univac in the U.S.A. . . ." (He's showing off in front of Albert.)

3. What does this sentence (page 30) tell you about Albert? "Albert's face was very red." (Albert was uncomfortable.)

4. What does this sentence (page 31) tell you about Albert? "I think I shall stay here and learn how to build a Univac." (Albert wants to belong.)

5. What does this sentence (page 36) tell you about Mrs. Smedley? "Would the Univac like a hamburger?" (She is glad that Albert is in the Univac. She has a sense of humor.)

Let a group or individual students select a character from the story and compile a list of quotations from the story which help develop that characterization. Follow this with a class discussion of the findings. Were there examples of conflicting emotions?

● It can be fun to put yourself in another's place. Ask pupils to suppose they were Albert inside the Univac. "Could you come up with answers as clever as his? What would you want to ask the Univac if you were the other characters?"

Have the pupils divide into groups of five each. Put this list of characters on the board and assign one to each person in each group.

Albert (Univac)	Mrs. Smedley
Rupert	Annabelle
Mr. Duncan	

Have each person make up questions that the character might ask the Univac and let the Univac answer each one. Switch characters so that everyone gets a chance to be the Univac. Have each group pick the four best questions and answers and share them with the class.

● This story is a good one for pupils to dramatize because the dialogue is lively and the plot is simple and fairly well defined. Help pupils choose the actors that will be needed and decide which scenes in the story they wish to dramatize. If there is time, they may bring in whatever ''props'' are available and build their own Univac.

Computers in Our World

(pages 252–257)

SUMMARY

Computers played a vital role in helping the operations director and the flight director guide the historic *Apollo 11* mission to the moon. Computers are not monsters; neither do they resemble humans. Computers can add, subtract, multiply, and divide. They also make comparisons, and obey instructions. Data processing (as for *Apollo 11*) and process control (for many kinds of manufacturing) are the two major areas of computer activity.

ABOUT THE AUTHOR

When he was only thirteen, Alfred Lewis decided that he would be a writer. He has written throughout his life, with the exception of his years as a lieutenant in the Merchant Marine during World War II. Before joining the staff of *National Petroleum News*, he served with other business publications. In addition to technical and scientific articles, he wrote the following books: *Clean the Air; This Thirsty World: Water Supply and Problems Ahead; Behind the Scenes at the Post Office;* and *The New World of Computers,* from which this selection is taken. Born in Boston, Mr. Lewis is a graduate of the University of California with a degree in psychology.

MATERIALS

- Sound filmstrip *The Computer at the Airport.*
- Satellite Book, *The Adventure of Flight.*
- Workbook pages 60–62.
- Evaluation Masters for "Computers in Our World."

HUMAN VALUES

- To develop an awareness of how computers work.
- To foster an awareness of the importance of computers in processing and storing the vast amount of information needed in a technological world.
- To stimulate thinking about the possible uses of computers for constructive or destructive purposes.

OBJECTIVES

The objectives listed below refer to specific skills for which lessons are presented in the Reading and Language section for this story. Many other skills are developed in Word Highlights, Interpretation and Comprehension, and through annotations. After reading the selection and participating in the discussion and activities, pupils should be able to demonstrate the following abilities.

1. To identify the noun referents of given pronouns.
2. To demonstrate strategies for decoding multisyllable words containing more than one medial consonant.
3. To demonstrate use of the suffixes *-ic, -al,* and *-ical.*
4. To identify and describe the meanings of given acronyms.
5. To distinguish between a dictionary, an encyclopedia, and an atlas in terms of the type of information each contains.
6. To identify the main idea and/or topic sentence of a paragraph.
7. To demonstrate and describe how information can be presented in different ways.

Teaching Strategies

WORD HIGHLIGHTS

1. Below is a list of etymologies from which certain space terms are derived. Explain meanings of terms if necessary. Copy the list on the board. Have pupils supply modern space terms.

Etymology	Term
a. *lift* plus *off*	lift-off
b. Greek *astron,* star, plus *nautes,* sailor	astronaut
c. Latin *capsula,* small box	capsule
d. *count* plus *down*	countdown
e. *blast* plus *off*	blast-off
f. L *spatium,* duration, plus OE *craeft,* strength or skill	spacecraft
g. L *orbita,* track, rut	orbit
h. *radio detecting and ranging* (acronym)	radar

2. Explain that the word *data* (in the story, *data* is used in the term *data processing*) is the plural form of *datum,* a loanword from Latin. English borrowed the word directly from the Latin and incorporated it unchanged. Write on the board these Latin loanwords that, like *datum,* form their plurals according to Latin rules:

alumnus — alumni	**antenna — antennae**
alumna — alumnae	**hippopotamus — hippopotami** (or -*es*)
alga — algae	

3. Have pupils determine the common element of meaning in the following words: *countdown, split-second, hour, ticking, minutes, timing.* (Time.)

4. Write on the board the following Glossary words and read them aloud with your pupils:

assemble	**complicated**	**meter**	**system**
calculation	**electronic**	**mission**	**tracking**
chemical	**mechanical**	**robot**	**transistor**
			veer

   Have one group of pupils copy these entries on individual file cards; have another group copy the Glossary definitions on individual file cards. Have the words and their definitions matched.

INTRODUCING THE SELECTION

What is the title of the essay you are going to read now? ("Computers in Our World.") Take a quick preview. What are the subtitles of the essay? ("Men into Space"; "Monster or Servant?")

Let's think about the second subtitle for a moment. Science has surrounded us with machinery and technology of many kinds. The computer is one kind of machine. When you think about some of the machines in your own home, in your school, or in your neighborhood, do they seem in any way to make life easier? Do they serve you? (Answers will vary.)

Now think about some of the by-products of modern technology. Inventors do not foresee many of the results of their inventions at the time they invent them. Can you think of any ways in which we might have been healthier and/or happier before certain inventions were around to help us? (A discussion may produce observations about such hazards as air pollution, water pollution, noise pollution.)

Under what circumstances might a computer be termed a monster? (If it were to stop working for people and instead began to control them.) You will find as you read that, so far, computers have served the needs of their masters in many ways.

GUIDED SILENT READING

Write the following on the board:

    I. The role of computers in the *Apollo 11* space flight
      A. Before blast-off
      B. (After blast-off)   Leave blank on board.
    II. The nature of computers
      A. Fact and opinion about them
      B. Their appearance
      C. (Their function)   Leave blank on board.

The outline I have written on the board is incomplete. Copy it and after reading the selection silently, fill in the blanks to complete the outline. Read carefully and think clearly as you do this.

Go over outlines after Interpretation and Comprehension.

Computers in Our World

ALFRED LEWIS

Men into Space

Back on July 16, 1969, a machine far from the scene of the lift-off played a key role in sending astronauts Neil Armstrong, Edwin Aldrin, and Michael Collins on their historic trip to the moon. In the early morning hours of that day, the three astronauts sat tensely in their Apollo capsule, *Columbia*, on top of a Saturn rocket. The countdown had begun. They were waiting for the final signal.

Would they be allowed to blast off? Or would there be a delay? Was everything in perfect order? Was it GO or NO GO?

An operations director at the control center at Cape Kennedy would make the decision. But his word depended on thousands of facts and figures. The director had to know about each of the engines, fuel lines, meters, and instruments on the spacecraft. He had to know about weather conditions in many different places. He had to be sure that the seventeen tracking stations around the world were in operation and that they would be in radio-telephone communication with the control center.

252

---

lift-off

Instant in which, or motion by which, a rocket begins flight. Also used popularly to denote beginning of other projects. Compare *blast off,* term for the launching of rocket or space vehicle. Both terms influenced by aircraft *takeoff.*

Apollo

Most influential of Greek deities. As god of the sun, Apollo provides an appropriate name for the U.S. space effort.

Typographical Clue

Columbia. Italics set off name of space capsule; also names of ships and aircraft. Compare *Apollo II,* page 253.

Saturn

Second largest planet in the solar system, named for mythical Roman king, whose reign was characterized as a golden age. Relate to *Saturday.*

countdown

Counting in reverse to zero launching time while checking equipment—a technique originated in a science-fiction film of the 1920's.

INTERPRETATION AND COMPREHENSION

GETTING THE MAIN IDEA

What historic event is being described here? (The first manned spaceflight to the moon.) Yet, as the first paragraph is written, neither the flight nor the astronauts take the place of importance. What is the main idea of the paragraph? (A machine played a key role in sending the astronauts to the moon.) In light of the subject of this essay, it is understandable that the author focuses on a machine. But can you reorder the sentences in the paragraph to give the astronauts a place of greater importance than the machine? (Begin the paragraph with the second sentence.)

USING IMAGINATION

Times change. In 1969 a moon flight was historic. What event might have been called historic a hundred years ago? What event might be called historic in the year 1980? (Answers will vary.)

No man or army of men could assemble all these facts at the moment needed. The operations director was assisted by a thinking machine—a computer. It was this machine that gathered and compared information to clear the lift-off at 9:32 A.M.

Another computer at Mission Control in Houston, Texas, was also ticking away its facts and figures as *Apollo 11* veered into orbit minutes later. Into the machine's "memory" came reports from around the world and signals from the spacecraft. From this information, the machine knew where the spacecraft was at any moment, where it would be ten or sixty minutes later. It could advise each of the tracking stations how to point its radar instruments.

Through such information, the flight director also knew whether the flight was going as planned. The thinking machine could help him make a split-second decision on whether the flight should continue. If something was wrong, the computer's calculations would control the timing for setting off rockets to slow the spacecraft down and start it back to earth. Only with this help would the astronauts be able to land on the moon.

Without such control and timing, none of the astronauts would have been able to make their pioneering space flights. Nor would they have been able to land at a planned spot, either on the earth or on the moon.

253

assemble
gather
Both words mean to bring together. *Assemble* means to bring together for a definite purpose while *gather* just means to bring together.

A.M.
From L *ante meridiem,* before midday. Compare P.M., *post meridiem.*

Punctuation Signal
"memory." Quotation marks are used because the machine's recall only approximates the highly complex activity of human memory.

split-second
Instant, immediate. Term originated from chronograph having two independently controlled second hands, one of which can be stopped for a reading and then made to catch up with the other. For accurate timing of more than one in a race.

During what part of the astronauts' mission did the first computer operate? (Prior to lift-off.) What were the two operations it performed? (Gathering and comparing information.)

After lift-off the operation of the second computer became of utmost importance. Where was it based? (Houston, Texas.) What kind of information did it record? (Reports from around the world; signals from the spacecraft.) What predictions could the computer make as a result of the information it had? (Where the spacecraft would be ten or even sixty minutes later.)

Once the spacecraft went into orbit, what would you say was the greatest responsibility of the flight director? (To decide from moment to moment whether the flight ought to continue.) How would the computer be essential in the event of trouble? (Its calculations would control the timing for the rockets that would slow the craft and enable it to return to earth.)

SKIMMING FOR IMPORTANT DETAILS

UNDERSTANDING TECHNICAL INFORMATION

MAKING A JUDGMENT

Monster or Servant?

What are computers?

In their short history, they have been called by many names. Some people talk about them as mechanical monsters that have taken over man's work. Others say they are servants of mankind. Writers sometimes refer to them as thinking machines, giant brains, robots, electronic brains and modern Frankensteins.

Computers are quite different from all of these. They are not monsters. Unlike robots or Frankenstein, they do not look at all like human beings. They have no arms or legs, nor do they have a heart or feelings or a real brain.

254

robot
From Czech *robota*, work, especially compulsory labor, servitude. Hence, a machine that can perform some human functions. Used in wider sense of someone who works mechanically but lacks soul.

electronic
From New Latin (NL) *electricus*, from Gk *elektron*, produced from amber by friction. Connotations of *instant*, *automatic*, *efficient*.

DISTINGUISHING BETWEEN
FACT AND OPINION

The author believes that many people have false ideas about computers. What are some of these mistaken notions? (Paragraph 2.)

Have pupils supplement a Glossary check of *Frankenstein* with their own store of knowledge about the famous monster.

In what ways does the author disagree with these mistaken notions? (Paragraph 3.) Do you support one side or the other? Explain why.

In appearance, they look more like rows of metal cabinets or lockers. Inside the metal walls, however, are hundreds of wires and vacuum tubes and transistors, as in many radios and TV sets, only much more complicated. Often they are not a single machine, but a system of several machines. Some of the largest of these systems can take up most of the space in a room larger than a school library. Other computers are no bigger than a typewriter placed on a desk.

To compute means "to count or to figure," and this is the main job of a computer. It adds, subtracts, multiplies, and divides. One of the largest of these thinking machines does so at the hard-to-imagine speed of 250,000 additions a second!

255

Punctuation Signals
hard-to-imagine. Hyphens link elements of adjectival phrase.

"250,000 additions a second!" Exclamation mark adds emphasis.

In external appearance, to what are computers compared? (The large ones are compared to metal cabinets or lockers; the small ones to typewriters.) How do they differ from those? (Paragraph 1.) Who will find the lines that tell us how large some computer systems are? (Lines 7–9.) How small others are? (Lines 9–10.) Can you replace the word *typewriter* with another that would give the same image of smallness? (Answers will vary.)

Perhaps it is surprising, after reading about the impressive performance of computers during the spaceflight, to learn exactly what their basic operation is. Who can tell us what that operation is? (To count or figure.)

MAKING COMPARISONS AND DISTINCTIONS

SELECTING APPROPRIATE VISUAL IMAGES

GETTING THE MAIN IDEA

Computers do more than compute, however. One of their talents is that they can compare one number with another. They can compare one name with an entirely different one, one meter reading with an earlier record. Because they can compare, they can also select and sort and obey instructions.

Computers are used for two general purposes: *data processing* and *process control. Data* is another word for information, and *processing* means "handling." This is just what computers do in such cases. They handle facts and figures. They do many different things with these facts and figures. They add and subtract, combine items in new ways, put names in alphabetical order, play word games, and solve difficult puzzles.

Process control computers go one step further than data processing. They not only dig out information; they use that information to control other machines.

Process control computers run chemical factories, power plants, cement and paper mills and manufacturing at other types of factories. The computers keeping an eye on *Apollo 11*'s flight were examples of data processing in operation.

256

GETTING THE MAIN IDEAS

Glancing at the first paragraph, who can say what ability, in addition to computing, makes a computer so useful? (Comparing.) And what does this ability permit the computer to do? (To select, sort, obey instructions.)

Skim this page. Who will tell us what the author identifies as the two general purposes of computers? (Data processing and process control.)

APPLYING TECHNICAL INFORMATION

Both of these purposes were being achieved when the computers operated during the 1969 spaceflight. Turn back and skim the essay. Who will point out exactly what technical functions the computers performed? (Pages 252–253: They gathered and compared information about fuel lines, meters, instruments on the spacecraft, weather conditions, the working of the tracking stations; they controlled the timing of rockets; they advised tracking stations on how to point their radar instruments.)

LAUNCH CONTROL CENTER, CAPE KENNEDY, FLORIDA

Reflections

1. What determined whether or not the Apollo astronauts would be able to blast off for the moon? How were all the data for this decision collected?
2. To what have computers been compared? How are computers different from each of these?
3. For what general purposes are computers used?
4. Given the definition of *to compute*, what do you think *computer* means? Now compare your definition with the one in the dictionary.
5. What do you think computers will be doing in the year 2000?

257

After a pupil reads the final paragraph aloud, have pupils take out their outlines of the essay. Check those items that required completion and have pupils explain why they made their choices. Guide them to understand why certain entries are more logical than others.

Have pupils look back at the pictures and say in what way they clarify the major points in the selection.

Suggest that pupils may want to read more about this subject in *The New World of Computers* by Alfred Lewis.

Questions 1–4 can be used for quick oral review of the selection. Question 5 requires imagination and can provide the basis for written reports.

READING AND LANGUAGE

I. READING SKILLS

OBJECTIVE 1

● **To identify the noun referents of given pronouns. (Syntax)**

Read page 254, substituting the word *computers* for the words *they* and *them* and *computers'* for *their*.

Why did the paragraphs I read sound strange to you? (The repeated use of the word *computers*.) Now read page 254 as it is written. Did this reading sound more natural? What made the difference? (The use of pronouns as substitutes for the word *computers*.)

Pronouns do a useful job in serving as noun substitutes in our language. To understand their meaning, we must understand what the pronouns refer to. Let's turn to page 252. In the first paragraph the author uses the pronouns *their* and *they*. What do these noun substitutes refer to? (The astronauts.)

In the third paragraph, to whom do the pronouns *he* and *him* refer? (An operations director.) The pronoun *they* in the last sentence? (Tracking stations.)

Duplicate or write the following sentences on the chalkboard and draw a line under the pronouns.

Draw two lines under the noun (and its determiner, if it has one) each underlined word stands for.

Example: Albert came to visit in Wakefield. I first heard about him at breakfast Thursday morning.

1. Computers do more than compute. They can compare one number with another.
2. The director knew whether or not the flight was going as planned. The thinking machine could help him decide whether the flight should continue.
3. Mothers are funny. Even a computer couldn't figure them out.
4. I have a laboratory at home. It cost hundreds of dollars.
5. "We are as smart as the Smedleys. Why would their child be a second Einstein, while ours dreams great dreams about a piano box in an alley?"

OBJECTIVE 2

● **To demonstrate strategies for decoding multi-syllable words containing more than one medial consonant. (Phonology)**

Write the following words containing two medial consonants on the board.

sys/tem	his/tory
cap/sule	fac/tory
sig/nal	fan/tasy

Study the first column and tell us what clues you see for decoding the words. (Two syllables, two medial consonants.) Underline the two consonants in each word. How many sounds do the two consonant letters stand for? (Two. Have pupils say the words and listen for the sounds if necessary.) How would you divide the words into syllables? (Between the two consonants: . . . C/C . . .) Now mark slashes for the syllable divisions.

Who will pronounce the words as separate syllables and then run the syllables together the way we normally speak? (Pupils should note that the syllable patterns for pronunciation, which may be written over the words, are CVC/CVC as in *sys/tem*.) What kind of vowel sound is in the first syllable? (Short, or unglided.) Why? (The syllable ends in a consonant; its pattern is CVC.) Where is primary stress? (On the first syllable.)

Proceed similarly with the second column and have pupils state a generalization about syllable division in words with more than one medial consonant. (When there are two consonants standing for more than one consonant sound in the middle of a word, divide between the consonants, giving the first syllable or syllable to the left of the division a "short" vowel sound. Primary stress is on that syllable.)

Remember that a single consonant between two vowels may be pronounced with the preceding or the following vowel. In *history*, *factory*, and *fantasy*, the *r* and *s* go with the following vowel, which is long because no consonant follows.

What is the vowel sound in the second syllable of the words in both columns? (Schwa. The stress pattern is '/ə.)

Present the following words with three medial consonants: *tremble, assemble, control, arctic*. Syllable division for the first three words is after the first consonant: C/CC. In *arctic*, division is after the second consonant: CC/C.

● **To demonstrate use of the suffixes -ic, -al, and -ical. (Morphology)**

Write the following sentences on the board.

> The words were arranged in alphabetical order.
>
> The mechanic fixed our car.
>
> She took part in many cultural affairs.
>
> Her arrival was unexpected.

Who will write on the board the base word and suffix for the underlined word in the first sentence? (Alphabet + -ical.) What does the suffix -ical mean in alphabetical in this sentence? (Relating to.) What does alphabetical mean in this sentence? (Relating to the alphabet.) Notice that -ical changed a noun to an adjective. The suffix -ical in alphabetical means the same as -ic in the variant form alphabetic.

Who knows what the base word is in mechanic? (Machine.) What is the suffix? (-ic.) What does the suffix -ic mean in mechanic in this sentence? (One associated with.) What does mechanic mean in this sentence? (One associated with machines.) Mechanic is a noun in this sentence.

Who will write on the board the base word and suffix in the underlined word in the third sentence? (Culture + -al.) Notice that the final e is dropped when you add an ending that begins with a vowel. What does the suffix -al mean in cultural in this sentence? (Relating to.) What does cultural mean in this sentence? (Relating to culture.) Notice that -al changed a noun to an adjective.

Who will write on the board the base word and suffix for the underlined word in the fourth sentence? (Arrive + -al.) What does the suffix -al in arrival in this sentence mean? (Act of.) What does arrival mean in this sentence? (Act of arriving.) Notice that -al changed a verb to a noun.

Duplicate and distribute the following exercise.

Underline the word in parentheses that best completes each sentence.

1. One of the Indo-European languages is ___

   (Iceland; Icelandic)

2. Such a law would not be in the ___ interest.

   (nation; national)

3. He was interested in any kind of ___ device.

   (electron; electronic)

4. The children sought the ___ of their teacher.

   (approve; approval)

5. The test included a comparison of ___ shapes.

   (geometry; geometrical)

● **To identify and describe the meanings of given acronyms. (Semantics)**

You have probably seen the term *NASA* in reference to the space program and the Apollo flights. Who knows what the individual letters N-A-S-A stand for? (National Aeronautics and Space Administration.) When a pronounceable word is formed from the initials of other words as this one was, what is it called? (An acronym.)

Radar is a word used in this essay. If you were to look up this word in a dictionary, you would find that *radar* is an acronym. The full term is *radio detecting and ranging*. Who will write this term on the board, underlining the letters that form the acronym *radar*? (Radio detecting and ranging.) Are all words or only the most important words represented in this acronym? (All.) Are only the initial letters of each word used? (No, *ra* comes from *radio*.) How does the appearance of the word *radar* differ from that of *NASA*? (*Radar* is written in small letters; *NASA* in capitals. Acronyms may be written either way.)

Divide the class into two teams and have pupils list as many acronyms as they can. Put the full terms on the board and ask opposing team members to identify the acronym. Some examples are the following.

> sound navigation ranging (sonar)
>
> self-contained underwater breathing apparatus (scuba)
>
> United Nations Educational, Scientific and Cultural Organization (UNESCO)
>
> United Nations International Children's Educational Fund (UNICEF)
>
> North Atlantic Treaty Organization (NATO)

● **To distinguish between a dictionary, an encyclopedia, and an atlas in terms of the type of information each contains.**

Discuss the various sources of information that are available in homes and in the school library.

Most people have a dictionary at home. What kind of information is found in a dictionary? (Spellings, pronunciations, and definitions of words.) In an encyclopedia? (Factual information on a variety of subjects.) In an atlas? (Statistics and maps of the world's continents and countries.) Where would you look to find the location of the capital of Texas? (In an atlas.) The spelling of *processing?* (In a dictionary.) The date of the launching of the first man-made satellite? (In an encyclopedia.)

Review the usefulness of knowing where to look to find the answers to specific questions.

Distribute the following exercise for independent practice.

A. Decide where you would look first to find the answer to each of the following questions. Choose either an atlas, a dictionary, or an encyclopedia and put **A** for atlas, **D** for dictionary, or **E** for encyclopedia in the blank after each number to indicate your choice.

1. Houston is situated northwest of what bay of water?   A

2. Who wrote the famous horror novel, *Frankenstein?*   E

3. Several planets have moons. Can you name three of them other than Earth?   E

4. Is Cape Kennedy on the east or west coast of Florida?   A

5. Which three states between Texas and Florida border on the Gulf of Mexico?   A

6. If someone called you an automaton, would he mean you are spirited or mechanical?   D

7. Who invented the first practical typewriter, and when was it patented?   E

8. What is the plural spelling of *memory?*   D

B. Answer the above questions by looking up the information in the source you chose.

OBJECTIVE 6

- **To identify the main idea and/or topic sentence of a paragraph.**

A group of sentences about one subject is a paragraph, and a paragraph usually has one main idea. Look at the first paragraph in the essay. What is the main idea of this paragraph? (A machine played a key role in sending the first astronauts to the moon.) Is the main idea stated in one sentence? (Yes.) Which one? (First.) What is a sentence stating the main idea called? (The topic sentence.) Does it always appear first in a paragraph?

T·442 (No, it can be anywhere, but it is usually first or last.)

Ask pupils to write the main idea of five paragraphs in the essay, using the topic sentence of the paragraph if there is one. Then let the pupils read their lists and give reasons if they disagree.

II. LITERARY SKILLS

OBJECTIVE 7

- **To demonstrate and describe how information can be presented in different ways. (Rhetoric)**

The following article contains some of the same information that you read on the first two pages of "Computers in Our World." See how they compare.

This article may be duplicated and distributed for pupils to read silently.

On July 16, 1969, astronauts Neil Armstrong, Edwin Aldrin, and Michael Collins began their historic 240,000-mile trip to the moon on the top of a Saturn rocket. Computers played a large part in each step of the operation, both at the control center at Cape Kennedy and at Mission Control in Houston, Texas.

The computer at Cape Kennedy provided many facts and figures about such things as instruments on the spacecraft, weather conditions in different places, and the condition of the tracking stations around the world. This information told whether or not the scheduled lift-off was possible.

After the rocket took off, the computer in Houston provided information that helped the flight director to know if the flight was going as planned and to decide at any time whether or not the flight should continue. The computer also made it possible for the astronauts to land at a planned spot, both on the earth and on the moon.

Everything went as planned, and on July 20 the astronauts made their successful moon landing. Five days later, on July 24, the command module splashed down in the Pacific Ocean.

Let's call "Computers in Our World" Version I and this article Version II. What general differences did you notice between the two versions? (The essential difference between the two is that the book version is much more dramatic and gives the computers the stature of heroes. Version II describes computers in a much more condensed, matter-of-fact way and focuses more attention on the astronauts themselves.)

After pupils discuss the two pieces in general terms, have them compare them, paragraph by paragraph, to find out why Version I is the more interesting one. They may write their findings.

Version I	Version II
1. The computer is highlighted. Suspense begins to build.	The astronauts and the flight are highlighted.
2. Suspense continues to build, emphasized by questions and capital letters.	The use of past tense removes all doubt as to the outcome of the flight.
3. Details make the reader feel that the computer is indispensable.	
4. This paragraph underlines the importance of the computer to the lift-off. The computer is is called a "thinking machine."	
5. Readers can visualize *Apollo 11* veering into orbit as the computer ticks away its facts.	The original fifth and sixth paragraphs are summarized, without the drama.
6. The expression "split-second decision" creates a feeling of danger and excitement.	
7. Page ends by focusing reader's attention on the computers.	The article ends by focusing the reader's attention on the astronauts and on the flight.

III. REGROUPING FOR INDIVIDUAL NEEDS

Reinforcement Activities

The following reteaching activities are suggested for use with pupils who had difficulty with the Evaluation Masters.

Objective 2: Help pupils mark syllable division between medial consonants in the following words from page 256 in the text.

1. compute	6. subtract
2. compare	7. combine
3. earlier	8. order
4. number	9. control
5. handle	10. further

Objective 3: For pupils who need additional help with the suffixes -ic, -al, and -ical, write the following words on the board and have pupils write the base word of each.

1. athletic	athlete	5. periodic	period
2. coastal	coast	6. refusal	refuse
3. historic	history	7. denial	deny
4. clinical	clinic	8. musical	music

Extension Activities

Objective 7: Have pupils collect various articles on the same news item from several different newspapers or periodicals. They may make notes on the differences in each, and compare their findings.

IV. ENRICHMENT

- Suggest that some people think the day is not too far off when every American may be able to own his own computer—or at least make use of a centralized computer headquarters. Have pupils enter a make-believe contest in which "first prize" goes to the writer of the best essay on the subject "How I Would Use My Very Own Computer."

- This essay may stimulate pupils' interest in computers. Encourage interested pupils to write some of the large computer manufacturers for information on the very latest computer technology. They can combine this information with some of their own imaginative thinking and report to the class on "Computers Today and Tomorrow."

- Some parents of pupils may be in industries which make considerable use of computers. This may be a good time to invite such a parent to talk to the class. This is also a good time to present the sound-filmstrip "The Computer at the Airport."

May Swenson

Miss Swenson is the recipient of numerous major awards and grants, including the National Institute of Arts and Letters Award (1960), the Shelley Memorial Award (1968), Guggenheim, Ford, and Rockefeller Foundation Fellowships. She brings to her poetry freshness of insight, precise imagery, and mastery of a variety of forms. Born in Logan, Utah, she is a graduate of Utah State University and now lives in Sea Cliff, New York. Among her poetry collections are: *Another Animal, To Mix With Time, Poems to Solve,* and *Half Sun Half Sleep.*

The Cloud-Mobile
MAY SWENSON

Above my face is a map.
Continents form and fade.
Blue countries, made
on a white sea, are erased,
and white countries traced
on a blue sea.

It is a map that moves,
faster than real,
but so slow.
Only my watching proves
that island has being,
or that bay.

258

THE CLOUD-MOBILE

Before introducing the poem, have pupils discuss shapes and forms they may have seen in clouds. Discuss the shapes and colors of clouds early in the morning, at sunset on a windy day, on a still, wintry day, or on an overcast day, during a thunderstorm, etc. Have a pupil read the definition of *mobile* from a dictionary and have the class discuss its several meanings. Ask pupils to read the poem silently relating the title to a specific meaning of *mobile.*

Have the poem read aloud. Then use the recording of the poem for another oral interpretation.

RECOGNIZING IMAGERY   Write on the board, "Above my face is a map." Discuss the imagery in the first stanza. Write, "It is a map that moves." Point out that *it* refers to the sky. Discuss the imagery in the second stanza, emphazing how rapidly the clouds may change in appearance.

Write, "It is a model of time." Discuss the imagery of the stanza. Suggest that

T•444

It is a model of time.
Mountains are wearing away,
coasts cracking,
the ocean spills over,
then new hills
heap into view
with river-cuts of blue
between them.

It is a map of change.
This is the way things are
with a stone or a star.
This is the way things go,
hard or soft,
fast or slow.

259

a clock is a model of time because it shows us the hours and seconds of a day. A calendar is a model of time, showing days, weeks, months, and years.

Is the earth, which shows changes from sea, wind, rivers, heat, cold, and motion, a model of time? How may a storm or a flood change the earth's appearance?

Write, "It is a map of change." Discuss the imagery of the last stanza.

How do stones change? How does a star change?

This is a sophisticated and philosophical poem, and may be read on several levels. By comparing the images with their own observations, the pupils will gain understanding and be awe-inspired.

"The Cloud-Mobile" is taken from A Cage of Spines by May Swenson. Suggest that pupils may want to read more poems from that book.

Robert H. Goddard: Father of the Space Age

(pages 260–264)

SUMMARY

Charles Lindbergh was instrumental in getting a $50,000 Guggenheim grant for Dr. Goddard, a professor of physics at Clark University, Worcester, Massachusetts, to continue his experiments with making a many-staged, liquid-fueled rocket. Roswell, New Mexico, was chosen as the best site. In the summer of 1930, Dr. and Mrs. Goddard and three assistants arrived to begin work on building the rocket and launching tower in Eden Valley, more than a dozen miles from town. The rocket, nicknamed Nell and weighing under fifty pounds, measured eleven feet in length and nine inches in diameter. In late December this rocket was shot two thousand feet into the air. This small beginning and countless subsequent efforts provided the basic principles on which our giant space rocketry program was founded. In 1961 NASA'S space center in Greenbelt, Maryland, was fittingly named the Goddard Space Center in honor of Dr. Goddard, space pioneer.

ABOUT THE AUTHOR

Educator and author, Clyde B. Moore was for many years professor of education at Cornell University. In 1948 he undertook major responsibility for preparation of Scribner's eight-volume *Social Studies Series*. Born in Albion, Nebraska, Dr. Moore is a graduate of Nebraska Wesleyan University. He received an M.A. degree from Clark University and a Ph.D. from Columbia University.

The Alfred E. Smith Award to Dr. Moore in 1950 was made in recognition of his outstanding service to the field of education. He has written numerous books and articles. This selection is taken from *Robert Goddard: Pioneer Rocket Boy*.

MATERIALS

- Satellite Book, *Spaceship Earth: Danger! Danger! Danger?*
- Workbook pages 63–64.
- Evaluation Masters for "Robert H. Goddard: Father of the Space Age."
  A large map of the United States.

HUMAN VALUES

- To stimulate an interest in the technical development of rocket fuel.
- To develop a realization of the time and effort that went into the perfecting of rockets.
- To appreciate the application of the pioneer spirit in various fields of endeavor.

OBJECTIVES

The objectives listed below refer to specific skills for which lessons are presented in the Reading and Language section for this story. Many other skills are developed in Word Highlights, Interpretation and Comprehension, and through annotations. After reading the selection and participating in the discussion and activities, pupils should be able to demonstrate the following abilities.

1. To identify and describe exceptions to generalizations about decoding two vowel letters together.

2. To identify and describe exceptions to generalizations about decoding syllable patterns.

3. To distinguish between words formed with base words and affixes, and words formed with roots and affixes.

4. To state the principle that most nouns change form to show a change in number.

5. To identify and construct irregular plurals of given nouns.

6. To identify and describe semantic relationships among given words.

7. To identify clues to setting, and to describe a given setting.

8. To match descriptive phrases and objects from a given selection.

Teaching Strategies

WORD HIGHLIGHTS

1. Have pupils locate the following places, which were important in the life of Robert Goddard. Use a large map of the United States for this exercise.

   a. **Worcester, Massachusetts,** where Goddard was a professor of physics at Clark University.
   b. **Roswell, New Mexico,** where Goddard did some of his most important work.
   c. **Eden Valley, New Mexico,** where Goddard's rocket-launching tower was built.
   d. **Greenbelt, Maryland,** location of a National Aeronautics and Space Administration space center.

2. Have pupils determine the meaning of the expression "many-staged, liquid-fueled rocket." (The phrase describes a rocket which consists of several stages or sections, each of which contains a propulsion unit carrying liquid oxygen fuel.)

3. Write on the board the following Glossary words. Have several science-oriented pupils explain these words.

aeronautics	**liquid oxygen**
atmosphere	**physics**
cylinder	**pressure**
experiment	**telescope**
igniter	**valve**

INTRODUCING THE SELECTION

Technological advances have made man's life on earth pleasanter and much more complicated. We can send images and sound through space. We can store, sort, and control vast amounts of information. Can anyone think of another invention of the last fifty years that may some day enable everybody to travel in space? (Rocketry.)

You are going to read a short biographical essay about a key period in the life of one man responsible for rocketry. Turn to page 260 to find out who he is. (Robert Goddard.)

GUIDED SILENT READING

As you read, make a list of the five main events described in the essay that took place after Dr. Goddard and his staff arrived at the site of their experimentation. We will discuss your lists later.

Robert H. Goddard:
Father of the Space Age

CLYDE B. MOORE

*Ever since he was a young boy, Robert
Goddard was interested in anything that zoomed
through the air. He learned all he could about
the planets and outer space. By the time he was
a professor of physics at Clark University in
Worcester, Massachusetts, he dreamed of making
a many-staged, liquid-fueled rocket. His first experiments at his Aunt Effie's nearby farm
angered the neighbors because of the noise and
the threat of fire. If he was to continue with his
experiments, he would need a more suitable lo-
cality to work in—and more money.*

*Goddard's good friend, Charles Lindbergh,
was able to get him a grant of $50,000 from the
Guggenheim Foundation. Roswell, New Mexico,
was picked as the perfect site for his work because of its warm climate and dry air, its light
rainfall and no snow, and its distance from any
close neighbors who might complain.*

*The crew Goddard took with him included his
wife, who was his official photographer; Henry
Sachs, his instrument maker; and Albert Kisk
and Larry Mansur, his close assistants. In the
summer of 1930, Dr. and Mrs. Goddard set out
for New Mexico by car. The equipment they
would need—a freight car full—was sent by rail.*

INTERPRETATION AND COMPREHENSION

What was Robert Goddard's special dream? (To invent a many-staged, liquid-
fueled rocket.) How did another great dreamer help to make Goddard's New
Mexican work possible? (Charles Lindbergh got him a $50,000 grant from
the Guggenheim Foundation.) Why might Lindbergh be in close sympathy
with Goddard? (Lindbergh, too, was a space pioneer.)

MAKING A CONNECTION

MAKING A JUDGMENT

Why do you think the Guggenheim Foundation thought Goddard was a good
risk? (His training in physics was impressive.)

MAKING INFERENCES

What did Goddard plan to use the $50,000 for? (To pay for the site of the
experiment, expenses for a staff of five, equipment.) Was Roswell, New
Mexico, a good choice of site? Why? (Because of its warm climate and dry
air, light rainfall, and distance from neighbors.)

Through the friendly help of the Roswell people, the Goddards were soon settled. They would live three miles from the town in an old house on the Mescalero Ranch. Eden Valley, where the launching tower was to be built, was more than a dozen miles away.

The Goddards drove out to see it. It was a desolate place, but the crew went to work with a will. Each of them was eager for success in the experiment. Each felt it was a pioneer adventure.

The workshop was started before the freight car loaded with tools and materials had arrived. It was to be sixty feet long—the same distance as from the pitcher's box to home plate on a baseball diamond.

The climate was mild. There would be no New England ice and snow during the coming winter. The crew would have constant good weather for working.

Dr. Goddard and his crew planned to build and test a small model of a rocket as soon as possible to learn if a large rocket could be made on such a pattern. Every point needed to be tested and retested. Dr. Goddard was eager to have a real test before the year ended. He asked the crew if it could be done.

Every member of the crew thought they should try it. They corrected flaws in the motor and tried not to overlook anything. By late December they had checked and rechecked every point. All

desolate
From L de-, completely, plus *solus*, alone. Relate *sole, solo, solitary*.

Idiom
"with a will." With determination.

Punctuation Signal
"—the same distance." Dash sets off explanatory phrase.

Goddard thought ahead. Can you find evidence of this? (He anticipated his needs in building a workshop to store equipment even before it had arrived; he avoided future problems by planning to build a small test rocket first.)

INTERPRETING BEHAVIOR

How are we helped to picture the length of the workshop? (By a baseball analogy: the distance from the pitcher's box to home plate on a baseball diamond.) Does the comparison make the distance more real? (Yes.) If the five people in Eden Valley were gathered to play a baseball game, what would they be part of? (A team.) Instead, what "group" word describes them? (Crew.)

APPRECIATING ANALOGY

NOTING A COLLECTIVE WORD

Can you imagine what some of Goddard's reasons might have been for not devoting the efforts of himself and his staff to working on the actual, full-size rocket immediately? (This would allow him to correct imperfections that might cause failure, danger to crew members, and wasted expense.)

PREDICTING OUTCOMES

Nell

Also Nellie. Diminutive forms of Helen or Eleanor.

Simile (sim′ ə lē)

"like a piece of delicate china"

"like the steel tower of a windmill"

"like a giant dart"

"like the tail of a fish"

Simile is figurative language in which a comparison is made with the words *like, as, as if.*

atmosphere

From Gk *atmos,* vapor, plus *sphaera,* sphere. Sphere of vapor. Relate *hemisphere, atmosphere, ionosphere.*

agreed that the test must be made immediately and eagerly awaited the result.

The rocket, nicknamed Nell, had to be moved from the shop to the launching tower, which was twelve miles away. It was carefully wrapped in blankets and lifted like a piece of delicate china, set on a smaller trailer, and snugly tied in place. A truck cautiously pulled the trailer over the sandy trail to the launching site.

The flight tower, which would guide the rocket in its takeoff, could be seen in the distance. At first glance it looked much like the steel tower of a windmill; however, no turning wheel could be seen. The tower was open at the top to let the rocket escape. The four steel supports were firmly anchored in concrete.

The rocket, looking like a giant dart, the kind thrown at a target, was about eleven feet long, twice the height of the average man. It was nine inches in diameter, about that of a luncheon plate. Its nose was a smooth, shiny cone, shaped to pierce the atmosphere easily. At the other end were balancing vanes, formed like the tail of a fish. These vanes were to keep the rocket on its course. They must hold firm and not be swished about as a fish's tail is flipped.

Inside the cylinder were many delicate parts. There were pipes, small tanks to hold gasoline and liquid oxygen, and a powerful motor. The total weight was less than fifty pounds.

262

Use annotations to explain the many similes used in describing the rocket.

UNDERSTANDING WHERE
SIMILE DOES NOT APPLY

Comparisons, such as similes, extend our understanding. But the two things compared are not meant to be exactly alike in every way. Look over the page again. Who will tell us the important way that each part of the rocket was not like the thing it is compared to? (Paragraph 1: the rocket would be much sturdier than delicate china; paragraph 2: the steel tower had no turning wheel and did not function like a windmill; paragraph 3: the rocket did not have a needlelike tip that would pierce; the balancing vanes were firm, not pliant.)

Who will read each of the three paragraphs aloud? Who will read aloud the paragraph that describes the interior of the cylinder?

Near the base of the tower was a dugout with a heavy trapdoor. From this safe place Albert Kisk could touch off the flight. Farther away was a shelter of sheet iron. Dr. Goddard and two crewmen would wait there.

All members of the crew were busy putting the rocket into perfect condition in the tower. Early in the afternoon Mrs. Goddard drove out in her car. As the official photographer, she was ready with her camera. Larry Mansur, with telescope and stopwatch, was at a safe distance to measure time and distance.

The valves and containers for gasoline and liquid oxygen were given a final check. Then the igniter was fired. The pressure rose to 200 pounds per square inch. (Think of a big man weighing 200 pounds resting all his weight on one leg of a chair.) The rocket was allowed to rise two inches. The pressure rose to 225 pounds. Then Dr. Goddard gave the signal, and Albert Kisk, from the dugout, released the rocket.

With a mighty roar the rocket moved up through the sixty-foot tower. Up it went, faster and faster, shrieking as it rose. In seven seconds it was four hundred feet above the tower. According to Larry Mansur's measurements, it reached a height of two thousand feet. An important part of Dr. Goddard's dream had come true—he had used liquid fuel to shoot a rocket into the air.

263

touch off
Technical meaning: to cause to explode, to fire. Now used in wider sense of triggering an action.

Punctuation Signals
"(Think of . . . leg of a chair.)" Parentheses enclose explanatory comparison that makes the scientific measurement understandable in everyday terms.

The moment everyone waited for had arrived. Various safety precautions were taken before the blast-off. What were they? (Dugout with heavy trapdoor, sheet-iron shelter.)

SKIMMING FOR IMPORTANT DETAILS

As far as we know, which of the crew members had specific responsibilities at this time? What were they? (Albert Kisk was to release the rocket, Mrs. Goddard was to photograph the event, Larry Mansur was to measure time and distance with his stopwatch and telescope.) Who wasn't accounted for? (Henry Sachs and Dr. Goddard.) What do you suppose Goddard was doing? (Supervising.)

MAKING AN INFERENCE

At what point did Goddard give the signal to fire the rocket? (When the pressure rose to 225 pounds.) Was the experiment successful? (Yes.) What was the rocket's highest altitude? (Two thousand feet.)

DRAWING A CONCLUSION

Figurative Language
"years slipped by"

ceremony
From L *caerimonia*, religion; *caerimoniae*, religious rites. Relate *ceremonial, ceremonious*.

dedicate
From L *de-*, intensive, plus *dicare*, to proclaim. To consecrate to the gods, to declare solemnly. Relate *abdicate, indicate, predicate. Dicare* provides a partial source also for *dictionary, diction, ditto, ditty, benediction, addition, condition, indication, indite*, and many other words.

Many years slipped by. Test after test was made. Some experiments failed and others succeeded. Goddard's test rockets soared less than two miles into space, but his genius, experiments, and dreams provided the principles on which the mighty program of space rocketry is founded today.

At Greenbelt, Maryland, the National Aeronautics and Space Administration has developed a large space center. In 1961 a ceremony was held to dedicate this space center to Dr. Goddard. It is now called the Goddard Space Center.

Reflections

1. What is meant by "a many-staged, liquid-fueled" rocket?
2. Why was Roswell, New Mexico, chosen for Goddard's experiments? Give as many reasons as you can.
3. How long ago did Dr. Goddard perform his first experiments near Roswell?
4. Why do you think NASA felt that Robert Goddard deserved to have a space center named after him? Do you agree with them? Why or why not?
5. The introductory note says that Charles Lindbergh helped Goddard get money for his experiments. For what is Charles Lindbergh famous? Why does it seem natural that Lindbergh and Goddard were good friends? (Think of some ways in which they were probably much alike.)

264

MAKING JUDGMENTS

Some people might say that Goddard's accomplishment was small. Why might they argue this? What do you say? How did the National Aeronautics Space Administration feel about Goddard's achievement? (Last paragraph.)

MAKING AN OUTLINE OF MAIN TOPICS

Let's go back now and see what you have listed as the five main events that took place in Roswell. (Pupils' lists should look something like this: 1) construction of workshop, 2) building of test model of rocket, 3) transport of rocket to tower, 4) putting rocket in the tower, 5) release of rocket.)

Suggest that pupils may want to read more about this selection in *Robert Goddard: Pioneer Rocket Boy* by Clyde B. Moore.

USING REFLECTIONS

Questions 1–4 provide material for an oral review of the selection. Question 5 gives an opportunity for group discussion.

I. READING SKILLS

OBJECTIVE 1

● **To identify and describe exceptions to generalizations about decoding two vowel letters together. (Phonology)**

Write the following words on the board and have them read.

$\boxed{e}$	$\boxed{ô}$	$\boxed{i}$
said	launch	been
heifer	broad	build
friend	cough	
threat		

$\boxed{u}$	$\boxed{ə}$	$\boxed{ü}$
touch	luncheon	good
	mission	

What is the same about all the words in the first column? (The $\boxed{e}$ sound.) In many words you know, two vowel letters together stand for a "long" vowel sound. What is tricky about pronouncing the vowel-letter combinations in these words? (They stand for "short" vowel sounds.) Let's review the other vowel sounds.

Columns are arranged according to one unglided sound. The sound symbols may be written above the columns if desired.

When you decode unfamiliar words with two vowel letters together, think of the "long" sound for the letters, and if this pronunciation does *not* make sense to you, try a "short" vowel sound. Check the Glossary or dictionary to be sure of pronunciation.

Write the words *poet, pioneer,* and *creation* on the board, underlining the letters oe, io, and ea.

How do the underlined vowel letters in these words differ from the ones in the words you have just studied? (They are pronounced with two separate sounds in two separate syllables.) What other words of this type can you suggest? (Idea, fuel, giant, etc.)

OBJECTIVE 2

● **To identify and describe exceptions to generalizations about decoding syllable patterns.**

Write the following words on the board, and have them read.

old VCC	come CVCe
post CVCC	done CVCe
mild CVCC	give CVCe

Look at the first column of words. Why are the underlined letters tricky to pronounce? (A final consonant cluster usually signals a "short" vowel sound. The vowel letters in these words stand for "long" vowel sounds.)

Write or have pupils write the syllable pattern next to each word.

Proceed similarly with the second column. The CVCe pattern usually signals a glided vowel sound. All these words must be learned as exceptions to usual English syllable patterns.

Note: Historically, final e was written to end words in v or to fill out a line of print as in *done*. The letter o in *come* was originally u and was written as o to avoid confusion with the following m. The u represented a glided sound which later became unglided. The final e was originally pronounced.

OBJECTIVE 3

● **To distinguish between words formed with base words and affixes, and words formed with roots and affixes. (Morphology)**

Write the words *untrue* and *telephone* on the board.

We have been studying the effects of prefixes and suffixes when added to base words and roots. Here is a base word with a prefix: *untrue*. How do we find out what this word means? (One way is to think about the meaning of the base word and the meaning of the prefix.)

Here is a Greek root with a prefix: *telephone*. How do we find out what this word means? (By combining the meaning of the prefix with the meaning of the root.) Now let us see if you can separate words formed with base words from words formed with roots.

Reproduce and distribute the following exercise.

Read the words in the list and write the ones formed with base words in Column 1 and those formed with roots in Column 2.

supervise	recheck	pitcher	reject
concur	eagerly	provide	faster
dislike	describe	overlook	assist
compose	report	friendly	trailer

T•455

Column 1	Column 2
recheck	supervise
pitcher	reject
eagerly	concur
faster	provide
dislike	describe
overlook	assist
friendly	compose
trailer	report

OBJECTIVES 4 AND 5

- **To state the principle that most nouns change form to show a change in number. (Morphology)**
- **To identify and construct irregular plurals of given nouns.**

Write the following sentences on the chalkboard. Ask pupils to study them to see how the underlined nouns in each sentence pair differ.

1. _Goddard_ traveled to New Mexico.

    The _Goddards_ traveled to New Mexico.

2. Our crew of _scientists_ took turns working.

    The _scientist_ on our team solved the problem.

3. George ordered one _hamburger_.

    The Univac ordered five _hamburgers_.

How many scientists took turns working? (A _crew_ suggests several or many.) How many solved a problem? (One.) How many hamburgers did George order? (One.) the Univac? (Five.) How did these nouns change in appearance to show more than one? (The letter _s_ was added.)

To some nouns an _es_ is added to show a change in number: _box_ to _boxes_, _tomato_ to _tomatoes_. Other nouns have spelling changes to indicate more than one: _gentleman_ to _gentlemen_, _child_ to _children_, _ox_ to _oxen_; but almost all nouns change form to show a change in number.

Write these nouns from the story and the sentences below on the chalkboard: _director, photographer, telescope, measurement, cylinder_. Have pupils demonstrate their understanding of singular and plural by suggesting forms of the nouns to fit the blanks in the sentence.

I brought only one ____ with me today, but will bring several ____ along tomorrow.

OBJECTIVE 6

- **To identify and describe semantic relationships among given words. (Semantics)**

Most words fit under many categories. Here are some ways the word _pecan_ could be classified: tree, plant, living thing, hard-shelled substance, food, borrowed word, word of Indian origin, a two-syllabled word. How else might you classify _pecan_? How would you classify _crocodile_ or _satellite_?

The exercises that follow may be duplicated for independent practice.

A. Below are groups of words that belong to our vocabulary of science and technology. One word or term in each line does not fit. Draw a line through that word or term. Think of a substitute that relates to science and technology. Write it in the space provided.

1. memory bank ~~piano~~ satellite fuel ____

2. calculate electronics ~~opera~~ experiment

    ____

'3. data ~~violin~~ laboratory process ____

4. igniter orbit ~~recital~~ spacecraft ____

5. telescope ~~orchestra~~ reflector magnetic

    ____

6. transmission aquanauts engineer ~~trumpet~~

    ____

7. transistor capsule aeronautics ~~flute~~

    ____

8. ~~bass-viol~~ radar physics cylinder ____

B. What is a category name for the words you've crossed out? (Musical terms.)

II. LITERARY SKILLS

OBJECTIVE 7

- **To identify clues to setting, and to describe a given setting.**

Skim pages 260, 261, and 262 of the essay about Robert H. Goddard to find words and phrases which give the reader clues to its setting. (Page 260: Roswell, warm climate, dry air, light rainfall and no snow, distance from complaining neighbors; page 261: three miles from town in an old house on the Mescalero Ranch, Eden Valley . . . was a desolate place, mild climate, no New England ice and snow, constant good weather; page 262: sandy trail to launching site.)

Which word from the text might best describe the scene? (Desolate.) Who will give us synonyms for this word? (Barren, lonely.) What other words can you think of to describe the area? (Rugged, dry, remote, desertlike, sun-baked, deserted.)

There are many things about the setting in Roswell which the author hasn't told us. What vegetation and wildlife was to be found? What colors could be seen in the natural surroundings? What sounds did the Goddard crew hear as it worked? at night? Were the hot sun and the clear air refreshing or tiring?

Imagine the answers to these and other questions about the setting, and write a brief paragraph in which you bring the setting to life.

OBJECTIVE 8

- **To match descriptive phrases and objects from a given selection. (Rhetoric)**

The following exercise may be written on the board or duplicated and distributed for independent practice.

A. Find a descriptive word or phrase from among those listed below to fit each of the numbered items, and write the letter of the word or phrase in the blank next to the item.

1. the entire rocket	b
2. the balancing vanes of rocket	d
3. the entire flight tower	e
4. the nose of the rocket	a
5. the top of the flight tower	c

a. smooth, shiny cone
b. twice the height of the average man
c. open at the top
d. like the tail of a fish
e. like the steel tower of a windmill

B. On page 262, last paragraph, the items inside the rocket are mentioned, but not described. Write your own adjectives and similes to create a vivid picture of each of these.

1. the pipes _____

2. the small tanks to hold the gasoline and liquid oxygen _____

3. the powerful motor _____

III. REGROUPING FOR INDIVIDUAL NEEDS

Reinforcement Activities

The following reteaching activities are suggested for use with pupils who had difficulty with the Evaluation Masters. The teacher should develop additional exercises as needed.

Objective 6: Have pupils examine the words presented in the exercise for this objective. They should group these words according to whether they relate to the categories of *computer science* or *space science*, as follows. Some words fit under both headings. Encourage discussion of the two categories.

Computer Science	Space Science
memory bank	satellite
calculate	fuel
electronics	laboratory
data	igniter
process	orbit
magnetic	spacecraft
cylinder	capsule
	physics
	experiment

Extension Activities

Objective 7: Have pupils select a story setting that they particularly enjoyed from one of the earlier selections and write a brief descriptive paragraph. They should be reminded to include sights, sounds, smells, weather, animal life, etc.

IV. ENRICHMENT

● This sketch of Dr. Goddard may stimulate some pupils to organize a "Rocketry Center" in the classroom. The "center" could feature model rockets built to scale, a brief written and illustrated history of rocket engines, and a simplified explanation (and, if time and space permit, a demonstration) of the principle of rocket propulsion.

● Help interested pupils organize a debate on an issue related to America's exploration of space. Pupils could debate the resolution: "The United States should widen the scope of its space exploration and continue to try to win all aspects of the space race."

Pupils should choose two teams. Instruct them to research their topics and, on the day of the debate, come prepared to present their side of the resolution. Allow each team a prearranged amount of time to present its argument. Then permit each team to rebut the other's case. When the debate is over, have the class decide which side presented the stronger case and won the debate.

● Have pupils pretend they are pioneers in a new field and need donations to carry on their research. Instruct them to write a letter to a make-believe foundation, asking for the money they need. Have pupils read their letters to the class who will then act as the foundation's governing board and decide whether to grant or turn down the pioneer's request.

If pupils prefer, they may choose to act as real pioneers, such as Columbus, Pasteur, Charles Lindbergh, or Dr. Goddard himself, and try to imagine what they would have said in such a letter.

By the Light of the Moon (pages 265–277)

SUMMARY

Years ago the changing phases of the moon governed people's activities. The Ekoi of East Africa have handed down a story to explain the creation of the moon and its phases.

Mbui, a kindhearted sheep, grew bananas while Etuk, a hardhearted antelope, grew cocoyams. Various animals begged food from them. But when a crocodile offered them a shining stone in exchange for one farm, only Mbui accepted the offer. He hung the stone over his doorway to shine for the whole world. After three days Mbui was starving.

One night Mbui saw a sky man in a tree gathering palm kernels with difficulty because it was dark. Since the antelope Etuk and all the other animals refused to give Mbui any food in return for the light from the stone, he gave the stone to the sky man, who returned to the heavens with it. He placed the stone in a box, so that it shone out from only one side. When toward the end of each month the sky people failed to bring food in exchange for the light, the owner covered the stone little by little until another supply of food was finally brought.

ABOUT THE AUTHOR

A native of Brooklyn, New York, Alfred Slote has been associated with the Television Center at the University of Michigan since receiving his B.A. and M.A. degrees there. He also attended the University of Grenoble, France, on a Fulbright grant. Books by Mr. Slote include *Air in Fact and Fancy*, *The Princess Who Wouldn't Talk*, *Strangers and Comrades*, and *Moon in Fact and Fancy*, from which this selection is taken. He has won prizes for his educational television programs.

MATERIALS

- Workbook pages 65–67.
- Evaluation Masters for "By the Light of the Moon."

HUMAN VALUES

- To develop an understanding of African culture through literature.
- To develop an awareness of the folktale as an expression of the needs and concerns of a people.
- To stimulate an interest in the varied explanations of the phases of the moon.

OBJECTIVES

The objectives listed below refer to specific skills for which lessons are presented in the Reading and Language section for this story. Many other skills are developed in Word Highlights, Interpretation and Comprehension, and through annotations. After reading the selection and participating in the discussion and activities, pupils should be able to demonstrate the following abilities.

1. To identify words with specified Latin or Greek prefixes.
2. To describe the shift in accentuation which occurs with the addition of the suffix *-ion*.
3. To demonstrate the use of pronouns in N-V-N sentences.
4. To construct expanded sentences by adding adjectives and adverbial phrases.
5. To describe character and motivation in a given selection.

Teaching Strategies

WORD HIGHLIGHTS

1. Write *phase* and *crescent* on the board and explain their respective etymologies to the group. *Phase,* which means a *stage in the development of the moon,* comes from a Greek word *phasis,* which means *phase of the moon.* Thus, *phase* has undergone no change in meaning over time.

    Crescent has changed its meaning from its earliest use. Its Latin root, *crescere,* meant *to increase or to grow.* When *crescent* came into Middle English, its meaning had narrowed to describe that aspect of the moon presented at any phase between the new moon and the first quarter and between the last quarter and the succeeding new moon. This is only one of the meanings of our modern English word, *crescent.* Draw the familiar crescent shape on the board.

    Have pupils explain these other terms which appear in the story: *new moon* (the moon's phase when its dark side is turned toward the earth); *full moon* (when the illuminated side of the moon is turned toward the earth); *half moon* (when half the moon is illuminated).

2. The pupils should become familiar with these words which appear in the folktale following the essay on moon lore. Write them on the board and have pupils pronounce the names with you.

Mbui (m bü′ē)	A name from the folktale.
Etuk (ē′tŭk)	A name from the folktale.
Ekoi (ē′koi)	Tribe of East Africa.
cocoyam (kō′kō yam′)	An edible root found in the tropics.
Akarram (ak′ə ram)	A river in East Africa.
python (pī′thon)	A large snake that kills its prey by crushing.
palm kernel (päm kėr′nl)	Seed of a palm tree that yields palm-kernel oil.

    All the above words are in the Glossary.

3. Several of the remaining Glossary words for this selection are the names of animals. Pupils should learn *antelope, bush cow,* and *crocodile.*

4. Have pupils define each of the following verbs with a facial expression: *bewildered, fascinate, hesitated, marveled.*

INTRODUCING THE SELECTION

People who make great scientific breakthroughs have to have an unusual degree of curiosity; without it, they might give up before they succeed. But everyone, scientist and nonscientist alike, is apt to have a certain degree of curiosity, not only about the world but about things beyond. Probably for as long as people have lived on the earth, their imaginations have been stimulated by the idea of outer space.

For centuries men thought that the sun, the moon, and the stars revolved around the earth. Can you see why they might have believed that? Doesn't your own experience seem to suggest that the earth stays in the same place under your feet while the moon and the sun change positions?

In the sixteenth century men began to consider the idea that the earth and the other planets revolve around the sun. Today we all accept this idea. Who knows how long it takes the earth to travel once around the sun? (Approximately 365¼ days.) The moon goes around the earth. It takes 27 days, 7 hours, and 43 minutes for a complete revolution.

Once men thought the moon gives off light, just as the sun does. But with the aid of the telescope that he invented, an early scientist named Galileo was able to take a better look. He found that the moon has no light of its own but simply reflects the light of the sun.

You have all noticed that the moon seems to change its shape. Who can explain this? (Give pupils a chance to explain.) The moon never changes its actual shape. The different phases of the moon—new moon, crescent moon, full moon—are the result of the changing position of the moon in relation to the sun, as the moon goes around the earth.

You are about to read an East African folktale, or myth, in which the origin of the moon is explained.

GUIDED SILENT READING

Before you come to the tale itself, you will read a short essay about some of the superstitions that men once held concerning the moon. See whether you have heard any of them before.

In the tale itself, animals rule the earth. See if you think they lived wisely. Which animal, if any, would you have been like under the circumstances?

In addition, assign the following questions to be answered before Interpretation and Comprehension.

● In what way was Mbui unselfish? (He gave food to all the animals who asked for it, and he sold his farm to get the shining stone that would provide light for the whole world.)

● Why did Mbui give the stone to the sky man? (Because his fellow animals did not appreciate it, and he thought the sky man would hang the stone in the heavens where all could see it.)

By the Light of the Moon
ALFRED SLOTE

Good Luck, Bad Luck

Today most of us are pretty used to the moon. There it is up in the sky—crescent or half or full. . . .

Years ago, though, people lived by the changing phases of the moon. They kept calendars and holidays by the moon. They planted seed in the spring's new moon and harvested in the autumn's full moon. The American Indian would not go hunting if the crescent moon's horns were tipped upward, for he believed that that meant dry weather, and he liked to hunt over moist ground where he could see tracks. And fishermen all over the world told the morrow's weather by the moon.

> If the moon rises pale, expect rain;
> If it rises clear, expect fair.

265

INTERPRETATION AND COMPREHENSION

Years ago, before it was possible to travel to the moon, men gave the moon an important place in their everyday lives. They observed its changing phases. Some of their observations were put to practical use; others were the basis for superstitious beliefs. What were some of the practical uses to which the moon was put? (It was a basis for measuring days, months, and years; it helped fishermen tell the next day's weather.) We still look to the sky for help in measuring time. How? (The sun is our measure.)

Which of the old customs mentioned on this page were based on superstition? (Planting and harvesting at the time of a full moon; hunting, according to which way the crescent moon's horns were tipped.)

DISTINGUISHING BETWEEN FACT AND SUPERSTITION

fortune

From L *fortuna*, chance, fate, from *Fortuna*, the Goddess of Chance. Relate *fortunate, misfortune, unfortunate*.

"go a-courtin'"

Phrase in vogue in America in earlier days. It meant to woo or to engage in social activities, leading to engagement and marriage. This a- prefix is still current in some dialect usage. The loss of final *g* is characteristic of a wide segment of American English. Compare *a-hunting, a-thinking*. The a- prefix gives emphasis to the word to which it is affixed. The a- prefix from Greek, as in *atonal*, gives negative meaning.

"hill folk"

Plural. (Compare *people*.) The plural form with final *s* is informal.

lunatic

From L *lunaticus* (from *luna*, moon), moonstruck, loony, mad; from the superstition that the violence of lunacy changed with the moon's phases. Relate *lunar*.

sickle

From L *secula* (from *secare*, to cut), sickle, an implement with semicircular blade.

For many people the moon long remained a mysterious heavenly body that could bring good fortune or ill.

It could bring you good luck if it was a new moon and you had silver coins in your pocket to jingle. A new moon was also the time to make a wish, take a trip, go a-courtin', cut your hair or your fingernails. If you had a wart you wished to get rid of, you rubbed your hand over it during a new moon.

But the moon could bring bad luck, too. If you saw a woman combing her hair in the light of the full moon, or if you planted seed during the full moon, you had bad luck. Also, if you happened to glimpse the new moon over your left shoulder or saw it reflected in a well, you would suffer ill fortune.

Some hill folk say that moonlight dulls razors. And years ago almost everyone believed that if you slept with moonlight on your face, you'd go crazy. Indeed, so many people believed this that we get our word *lunatic* from the Latin word for moon, *luna*.

Today, of course, we know that none of these things is true. You can sleep in the moonlight and wake up as normal as you were yesterday. You might harvest your crops in the full moon with poor results or harvest in a sickle moon and do well. You might start your vacation during the new moon and have a flat tire right away.

266

SKIMMING FOR IMPORTANT DETAILS

Who will read the lines that tell about superstitions based on the idea that the moon brought good luck? (Paragraph 2.) That the moon brought bad luck? (Paragraphs 3 and 4.)

EXTENDING KNOWLEDGE THROUGH RESEARCH

Has anyone heard of any other moon superstitions? Who would like to find out more about moon myths and superstitions and tell the class about them?

Have the last paragraph read aloud; see annotation for *sickle*.

Nevertheless, there it is . . . the moon, hanging up there in the sky, seeming to change its shape before our very eyes. No wonder man continues to be fascinated by it. Since the beginning of time, he has sought to explain how it got there and why it behaves the way it does.

The first people to try to explain the creation and behavior of the moon were tribal poets and storytellers. There are hundreds of folktales that explain how the moon came into the sky and why it changes its shape. One story, told by the Ekoi people of East Africa, not only explains the origin and phases of the moon, but tells us why we see only one side of the moon.

267

Punctuation Signal
"there it is . . . the moon." Ellipses denote pause in thought and a sense of mystery beyond words.

origin
From L *oriri*, to rise especially with reference to sun or moon. The root produces *orient*, *oriental*, *original*, *originality*, *originate*, *disorient*, *aboriginal*, and other forms.

Read the first paragraph silently. Now try to recall the first paragraph in this selection. Do the two seem to be contradictory? (Yes.)

Who will read the second paragraph aloud so we can share an appreciation of what the myth explains?

MAKING A COMPARISON

GETTING THE MAIN IDEAS

python
From Gk *Puthon,* in mythology a monstrous serpent who lived in the caves on Mount Parnassus and was slain by Apollo at Puthō (ancient name for Delphi). Now means a genus of large, non-venomous snakes.

"Now . . . ."
Storytelling technique to focus attention as narrative resumes.

A Gift from the Python

Now all this took place long, long ago, before there were men on earth, when men lived in the sky, and the animals ruled the earth. Mbui, a kindhearted sheep, was one such animal; another was Etuk, a hardhearted antelope.

Both Mbui and Etuk were hardworking farmers. Mbui grew banana trees, and Etuk grew cocoyams. When the two friends got tired of eating the same foods, they would exchange and eat each other's food. When the bananas got too soft, Etuk the antelope would demand angrily that Mbui fetch him some fresher bananas, and kindhearted Mbui always did so.

One day while Mbui was fetching fresh bananas, he met a crowd of apes. Being hungry, they begged Mbui for some bananas, and the kindhearted Mbui gave them some.

NOTING CHARACTERS | Which animal characters are introduced to us on this page? (Mbui, a sheep; Etuk, an antelope.) What is their occupation? (Farming.)

LOCATING ADJECTIVES THAT CHARACTERIZE | They are both described by particular adjectives. Which one characterizes Etuk? (Hardhearted.) Mbui? (Kindhearted.) both? (Hardworking.)

MAKING AN INFERENCE | They are referred to as friends, but from the very beginning, the friendship seems unequal. Who will find the lines that show this? (Paragraph 2.) Do you think Mbui has to obey Etuk's demands? Why do you suppose he does? (It isn't in his nature to refuse.)

IDENTIFYING AUTHOR'S PURPOSE | Who can tell us in which paragraphs on this page the background for the story is given, and in which paragraph the action begins? (Background is given in the first two paragraphs; the action begins in the third paragraph.)

The apes ate their fill and went their way. Soon they met a herd of wild pigs, who saw how well fed the apes looked, and, being hungry themselves, they asked the apes where they got their food.

"From Mbui the sheep," said the apes.

Whereupon the pigs went to Mbui and begged for some bananas, and the kindhearted Mbui gave them some.

The pigs ate their fill and went their way. Soon they met an elephant, who saw how well fed the wild pigs looked, and, being hungry himself, he asked the pigs where they got their food.

"From Mbui the sheep," said the pigs.

Whereupon the elephant went to Mbui and begged for food, and, of course, kindhearted Mbui gave him some, too. He gave him great bunches of bananas, and he even got Etuk the hardhearted antelope to give the elephant five baskets of cocoyams.

And so, in time, all the bush beasts, even the bush cow, came to the two farmers, but especially to Mbui, and received food.

Now, not far from the farms of Mbui and Etuk was the great river called Akarram. In the midst of this river, deep down, dwelt the crocodile. One day the bush cow went to drink by the river and struck up a conversation with the crocodile.

"You look well fed, Cow," said the crocodile.

"I am," said the bush cow.

269

Idiom
"ate their fill." Ate enough to satisfy them. Compare "have their fill"; "to become sated or weary"; "to have enough or too much."

"In the midst . . . ."
Now chiefly replaced by "in the middle."

Alliteration
"deep down, dwelt the crocodile"

crocodile
From Gk *kroke*, pebble, gravel plus *drilos*, worm. Literally worm of the pebbles, from its habit of sunning itself.

Etuk is not the only animal to whom Mbui is generous. Skim the page. Who will tell us what other kinds of animals he feeds? (Apes, pigs, an elephant, a bush cow, all the other beasts.) Can you find evidence that Etuk also can share? (Paragraph 6.) Which paragraph summarizes the farmers' behavior? (Paragraph 7.) Do you believe that the generosity displayed has to come to an end sometime? (With care and luck, crops can be replenished and shared indefinitely.)

But the plot takes a new turn. With which word does the twist in the plot begin? (Paragraph 8: now.) Remember that folktales were originally told, not read. What effect do you feel the word now has on a listener? Listen, while I read the sentence aloud.

Read the sentence aloud, emphasizing *now* so that it conveys the message, "Listen very carefully to what I'm about to tell you."

SKIMMING FOR IMPORTANT DETAILS

RECOGNIZING PLOT DEVELOPMENT

Punctuation Signal

farmers—. Dash signals elaboration or explanation to follow. Compare last paragraph, page 273.

"Where do you get your food?"

"From those two busy farmers—Mbui the sheep and Etuk the antelope."

Well, no sooner did the crocodile hear this than, naturally enough, he crawled out of the water and went to Mbui and Etuk and said, "I am dying of hunger. Please give me food."

Etuk the antelope drew himself up. "To the animals who are my friends, I may give food, but to you I will give nothing, for you are no friend of mine."

But Mbui the sheep, who was kindhearted, shook his head. "It is true I do not like you either, Crocodile, but I will give you one bunch of bananas."

270

UNDERSTANDING CHARACTERS With what gesture does Etuk express his attitude toward the crocodile? (He draws himself up, indicating his antipathy toward the crocodile.) Yet there is one word in his reply to the crocodile that suggests that he is not wholeheartedly generous even with his friends. What is that word? (May.)

Even kindhearted Mbui dislikes the crocodile. Why do you suppose that is? (He is an enemy and probably a menace.) Can you think of any animal that the crocodile might fear? (Answers will vary.)

USING PICTURE CLUES Identify the animals in the picture on this page.

EXTENDING CONCEPTS You might discuss the concept of the animal as predator: most animals are both potential victims and potential threats to certain other animals.

T·468

The crocodile took the bananas and said, "Don't lock your doors tonight, farmers, for I will return and buy more food from you at a great price."

Then the crocodile returned to the river with his bananas and sought out the great python who lived there. The python had something very precious, and the crocodile knew about it.

"I have found two farmers who have much food," the crocodile said to the python.

"I am also very hungry," said the python. "Will you give me something to eat?"

The crocodile gave him a few bananas. When the python had tasted them, he sighed and said, "How sweet they are. Will you go back and bring me some more?"

"Yes," said the crocodile, "but will you give me something to buy bananas with?"

The python hesitated, and then he nodded, "Yes, I will give you something so valuable you can buy the whole farm with it."

And so the python did an extraordinary thing. He took from within his head a great shining stone and gave it to the crocodile. The crocodile took it and started to go back to the farm. Slowly he went, and night fell and the road grew dark, but he held in his jaws the shining stone, and it made a light on his path, and the way before him was bright. When he came near the farm, he hid the stone beneath his claws and called out.

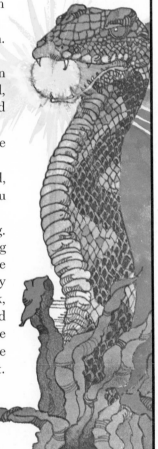

Paragraph 8
Style imitates the crawling motion of the crocodile. For example, sentence four contains five short, parallel sections—suggestive of the turns as the crocodile weaves his way along.

Read the first paragraph silently. When the crocodile says, "Don't lock your doors tonight, farmers, for . . .," do you suppose he means exactly that? What message is he really giving Mbui and Etuk? (It is his way of saying, "Expect me back soon.")

INTERPRETING LANGUAGE

Whom does the crocodile seek out at the river? (The python, select a pupil to check the Glossary for its meaning and report to the class.)

SKIMMING FOR IMPORTANT DETAILS

Skim the rest of the page. Who will tell us where the scene between the crocodile and the python ends? (Pupils should find the most logical place, somewhere within the last paragraph; have them give reasons for their choice.)

What can you gather from the fact that the python is willing to give away his precious stone for a banana farm? (Hunger must have been a pressing problem among the Ekoi people of East Africa; explain that in most parts of the world, people cannot take food for granted.)

UNDERSTANDING A PEOPLE THROUGH FOLKTALES

"Come out, Mbui the sheep. Come out, Etuk the antelope. I have something very valuable for you."

It was dark when the two farmers came out to speak with the crocodile, but slowly the crocodile opened his claws, and he held up the stone. It began to gleam, and when he held it up high, the whole land became so bright that you could see a needle or a pebble or any small thing. The crocodile then said, "The price of this that I bring from the python is one farm."

Etuk the antelope frowned and said, "It would be stupid of me to sell my cocoyam farm for a great shining stone like that. What good will that shining stone be to me if I starve to death?"

But Mbui the sheep loved the stone. "I will buy the python's stone," he said. "I will give you my whole farm of bananas, for that stone from the python lights up the whole earth. Take my farm. Take all of it, but let me have the great shining stone so that when darkness falls, the whole earth may still be light."

And so the exchange was made.

And Mbui went to his house and placed the stone over the doorway so that it might shine for the whole world. Etuk the antelope, on the other hand, shut his door and went to sleep.

Well, in the morning Mbui was hungry, and he had nothing to eat. He was hungry in the afternoon, and he had nothing to eat. He was hungry

"Mbui was hungry . . . ."
Note effectiveness of repeating phrases in paragraph.

272

RECOGNIZING SUSPENSE The crocodile takes his time in revealing the stone to the two farmers. Why? (Gradual exposure creates suspense.) Which phrase indicates just how bright the stone's light is? (". . . you could see a needle or a pebble or any small thing.")

COMPARING CHARACTERS What do the different reactions of Etuk and Mbui tell you about them? (Etuk is selfish, Mbui is generous; Etuk is practical, Mbui is impulsive.) Which of the two is more farsighted? (Answers will vary.)

at night and hungry the next day. He had nothing to eat, for he had sold his farm for that great white stone.

On the third day of his hunger, Mbui asked Etuk the antelope for a single cocoyam, but Etuk said coldly, "I will give you nothing, Mbui, for you have nothing to give me in exchange. Did I tell you to buy that shining thing? To give something when you have a lot of it is good, but who but a fool would give everything he has so that a light may shine in the dark!"

Poor Mbui was bewildered and upset. "I have done nothing bad," he thought. "Before, no one could see in the night. But now the python's stone shines so that everyone can see and choose his path at night."

That very night, weak with hunger, Mbui dragged himself down to the riverbank to drink. By the riverbank he saw one of the sky men— those lords of the sky who come down to earth to gather food. This sky man was up in a tree trying to gather palm kernels, but he was having a hard time because it was so dark.

273

"a single cocoyam"
Oneness is emphasized by use of "a single"; Mbui asked for *only one* cocoyam.

coldly
Expressive adverb.

Read silently the last paragraph on the previous page, ending on this page. Do you think the idea contained in these lines is expressed in the briefest way possible? (No.) How can you rephrase the paragraph to make a briefer statement? (". . . Mbui was hungry for two whole days because he had sold his farm for that great white stone.")

Yet the idea is expressed in four sentences to create a certain effect. Who will read the paragraph aloud? Can anyone help us to appreciate the style of the paragraph? (The narrative style is pleasing to the ear, and it emphasizes the tediousness of two days without food.)

Etuk makes clear when he feels it is right to give, and when it is stupid. Who will read his lines aloud? (Paragraph 1.) What is Mbui's reply? (Paragraph 2.)

Pupils might like to give their own viewpoints on when it is wise to give and when it is not.

RECOGNIZING AND EVALUATING STYLE

SKIMMING FOR IMPORTANT DETAILS

DISCUSSING PERSONAL REACTIONS

"O Lord of the Sky"
Epithet suggests supernatural power
as a contrast to "people on earth."

Mbui called out to him. "It is useless to do such a thing in the dark, O Lord of the Sky. Are you blind?"

The sky man answered, "I am not blind. Why do you ask such a thing?"

"If you are not blind, I beg you to throw me only one or two palm kernels, and in return I will show you a thing more bright and glorious than any you have seen before."

The sky man threw down three palm kernels, which Mbui quickly ate. Then the sky man climbed down with great difficulty since it was dark, and together he and Mbui went to Mbui's house.

Mbui said, "Will you wait there a little while, Lord of the Sky, while I question my friends?"

"I will wait," said the sky man.

Mbui the sheep went to his friend Etuk the antelope and asked, "Will you not give me a single cocoyam to eat? The great python stone which I bought at the price of all that I had turns darkness to light for you, but as for me—I die of hunger."

Punctuation Signal
"as for me—I die of hunger." Dash
for sudden dramatic effect.

274

INTERPRETING DIALOGUE — Why do you think Mbui asks the sky man whether he is blind? (Not simply because he is picking kernels in the dark, but probably because Mbui wants someone else to appreciate the stone; if the sky man isn't impressed by the stone, Mbui implies that he will be acting like a blind man.)

INTERPRETING ACTION — Is there anything in the sky man's action in the fourth paragraph that suggests a generosity at least greater than Etuk's? (He throws down one kernel more than Mbui requested.)

RECOGNIZING MOTIVATION — Who will find the lines that tell whether Mbui planned from the first to give the stone to the sky man? ("... I will show you. ...") What do you suppose would prevent him from giving the stone away? (A sign from his friends that they care about him and admire the powers of the stone.)

Etuk said, "I will give you nothing. Take away your python stone for which you foolishly sold everything, and we will stay in our darkness as we did before."

Then Mbui asked all the other animals if they would give him just a little food in return for the light he had bought for them, but they all refused.

So Mbui went to his house and took the great shining stone down from the doorway and gave it to the sky man.

"I love the animals, but they do not love me," Mbui said. "Take the shining thing and go back from where you came. I know that you are one of the sky people. When you arrive home in the heavens, hang up my stone in a place where all of the animals on earth may see it shining and be glad."

The sky man took the stone and went back to the palm tree. He climbed the tree, higher and higher, pointing to the sky, and the tree lifted its branches and lifted him till, from its very top, he could climb into heaven.

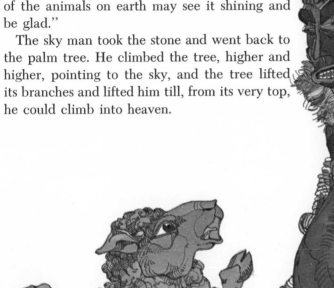

Last Paragraph
Style of paragraph suggests climbing.

Is the darkness to which Etuk refers in the first paragraph only the darkness of night? Do you think the animals are in darkness in another way? (The darkness from which they suffer results from their hardheartedness, as well as from their failure to imagine how the world would be enriched by the light of the stone.)

UNDERSTANDING SYMBOLIC LANGUAGE

After the animals have refused Mbui any food, although he is starving, does he act to hurt them and collect revenge? (No, he makes a gesture of extreme generosity.)

UNDERSTANDING A CHARACTER

Who will read aloud the lines that reveal the sky man's supernatural power? (Last paragraph.)

SKIMMING FOR IMPORTANT DETAILS

"Behold."
Biblical diction.

When he reached his home, the sky man called all the other men of the sky and spoke to them.

"With me I have something very precious and beautiful. It can shine so that all the earth will be light. From now on everyone on earth or in heaven will be able to see at the darkest hour of the night."

The sky lords marveled at the stone, and they decided that such a precious stone needed a box. But when they put the great shining stone in the box, it could only shine out from one side.

The sky man who had got it from Mbui took the box and said, "Behold. This stone is mine. From this time on, all the sky people must bring me food. I will no longer have to look for any myself."

Because he was the owner of the great shining stone, they brought him food. But sometimes they got tired and didn't bring him any. Then the sky man would cover the side of the box so that the stone could not shine until they brought him some. He would cover it just a little, and then a bit more, and then he would cover it all until they brought him food.

That is why the moon is sometimes dark, and then people on earth say, "It is the end of the month. The sky people have grown tired of bringing food to the owner of the great shining stone, and he will not let the stone shine out till they bring him a fresh supply."

supply
From L *sub-,* from below, up, plus *plere,* to fill. Relate *comply; supplement. Plere* provides a root for *plenty, plentiful, accomplish, incomplete, compliment, supplement, implement,* and other words.

276

GETTING THE MAIN IDEAS   In what way does the sky man demonstrate greater wisdom than the animals? (Paragraph 2.) This explains mythologically how the moon got into the sky. Who can tell us what remains to be explained before the tale is over? (The reason why we never see more than one half of the moon and why the shape of the moon changes during different times of the month.) Which paragraph offers an explanation for the first observation? (Paragraph 3.) the second? (Paragraph 5.)

MAKING AN INFERENCE   What does the description of the sky man's behavior in the fifth paragraph say about his character? (He is selfish, lazy, and power-hungry.)

The old African folktale is as much about hunger as it is about the moon. But the Ekoi storyteller, in trying to explain the universe to his people, was doing, in a sense, what scientists do today: seeking to explain the universe.

Reflections

1. The Ekoi people of East Africa believed that once, long ago, animals ruled the earth. But did these animals behave like animals you know? Support your answer with examples from the legend retold here.

2. What are superstitions? Tell some that you know and explain why you think they started.

3. Give at least two reasons why primitive people might be likely to have more superstitions about the moon than about the sun.

4. Think about the two statements below. In what ways might each of them be true?
   a. Primitive legends and myths were the first step toward knowledge.
   b. Primitive legends and myths tended to keep people from learning the facts.

5. What do we know about the moon today? In what ways did man get this knowledge?

277

universe
From L *uni-*, one, plus *versus*, turned with one impetus; literally, turned into one. The whole world, the entire body of existing things and phenomena. Relate *adverse, converse, reverse, subversive; universal verse, versatile, vertigo, vertebrate, version.*

Pupils will enjoy taking turns reading parts of this tale aloud. Have them go through the story again to locate logical scene shifts, and then assign sections to various pupils.

Suggest that pupils may want to read more about the moon in *Moon in Fact and Fancy* by Alfred Slote.

Question 1 can be used for a quick oral review of the selection. Questions 2–5 provide good material for group discussion.

RECOGNIZING A CHANGE OF SCENE

USING REFLECTIONS

READING AND LANGUAGE

I. READING SKILLS

OBJECTIVE 1

● **To identify words with specified Latin or Greek prefixes. (Morphology)**

Review the Greek and Latin prefixes in "Finding Patterns in Words," pages 283–284 of the pupil's text. Duplicate and distribute the following exercise.

Read the words and sentences below. Find a word in the list that completes each sentence. Write the word in the blank.

prehistoric	transcontinental	perforate
replants	submarine	circumscribe
exhale	repay	hypersensitive

1. A railroad that goes across a continent is a transcontinental railroad.

2. The time before recorded history is prehistoric time.

3. When a farmer plants a crop again, he replants it.

4. A boat that travels under water is a submarine .

5. To put holes through is to perforate .

6. To pay back is to repay .

7. To breathe out is to exhale .

8. To draw a line around is to circumscribe .

9. To be more sensitive than the average person is to be hypersensitive .

OBJECTIVE 2

● **To describe the shift in accentuation which occurs with the addition of the suffix -ion. (Phonology)**

Write the following on the board for pupils to copy or have it duplicated.

fascinate	fas′	fascination	na′
hesitate	hes′	hesitation	ta′
dedicate	ded′	dedication	ca′
calculate	cal′	calculation	la′
complicate	com′	complication	ca′

Study the first word in each column. What is the difference between them? (*Fascinate* ends in silent e and has three syllables; *fascination* ends in the suffix *-ion* and has four syllables.) Who will say the words aloud? Where is the primary stress in *fascinate?* (On the first syllable.) in *fascination?* (On the third, or the syllable before the suffix *-ion.*)

Write the syllables with primary stress in the spaces.

Which word, *fascinate* or *fascination,* is likely to be used as a noun in sentences? (Fascination.) Why? (It ends with the noun suffix *-ion.*) Who can give an illustrative sentence? (For example: "He watched the moon with fascination.") How do you think *fascinate* is likely to be used? (As a verb. Have pupils think of a sentence with the word *fascinate* and then analyze its use; for example: "The movie will fascinate you.")

Proceed similarly with the other words. Then ask pupils to formulate a rule or generalization for primary stress in related words when they are used as verbs or as nouns ending in *-ion.* (When the noun suffix *-ion* is added to verbs, primary stress is on the syllable before the suffix.) Other noun suffixes causing the same stress pattern to occur include *-ity, -ian* as in the words *electricity, musician.*

OBJECTIVES 3 AND 4

● **To demonstrate the use of pronouns in N-V-N sentences.**
● **To construct expanded sentences by adding adjectives and adverbial phrases.**

Write on the board the pronouns and sentences below.

I	you	we	he	they	it

1. Mbui waited.

2. The Indians planted seeds.

3. Fishermen made forecasts.

4. Mbui and Etuk farmed.

5. The crocodile summoned Mbui and Etuk.

6. Folktales explain the universe.

We have worked with a number of pronouns, or noun substitutes, in this unit. Today we will work with some others. Who will underline the noun markers and nouns and connectors in these sentences? What pronouns from the list can we substitute for which of these nouns? (1. he, 2. they, 3. they, 4. they, 5. it or he, 6. they.)

These pronouns fit the *first* noun position in Noun-Verb-Noun sentences or for the noun in Noun-Verb sentences.

Write these pronouns on the board beneath the sentences.

them   her   him   me   it   us

What substitutions can you make using these pronouns? (2. them, 3. them, 5. them, 6. it.) These pronouns fit the *second* noun position in the Noun-Verb-Noun sentences.

To provide practice in understanding longer sentences, write the following prepositional phrases on the board. Have pupils rewrite the sentences above in a more interesting form, adding these prepositional phrases and appropriate adjectives.

in the moist earth	at that time
until dark	in the light of the moon
by the moon	during the full moon

II.   LITERARY SKILLS

OBJECTIVE 5

● **To describe character and motivation in a given selection.**

Most of the characters in "By the Light of the Moon" are animals. Which of the animals has the most material wealth? (Some pupils may pick Mbui and Etuk because they have food while others are hungry; others may name the python, with his valuable stone.) How do we know that the python does not have everything he wants, even with his precious stone? (Because he asks the crocodile for food.)

Which animal do you suppose is the most widely disliked? (The crocodile.) Can you guess why the people who told this tale might have picked the crocodile to be the unpopular one? (Probably because it is a very dangerous and treacherous animal.)

Which of the animals do you feel most sorry for? Why?

(Mbui is the only really sympathetic character.) Whom do you like least? (Pupils may choose Etuk for his hardheartedness or the crocodile for making such an exchange or all the animals for forsaking Mbui after he had helped them so many times.) Do you think the price of the stone was too high for Mbui to pay?

Who are the nonanimal story characters? (The sky men.) Do you think they are kinder or wiser than the animals?

Present the following to the class.

Pick five of the following traits; and, in a few sentences, explain how each one plays an important part in the story.

hunger	selfishness
fairness	need
gratitude	cleverness
foolishness	love of beauty
hardheartedness	kindheartedness

III.   REGROUPING FOR INDIVIDUAL NEEDS

Reinforcement Activities

The following reteaching activities are suggested for use with pupils who had difficulty with the Evaluation Masters. The teacher should develop additional exercises as needed.

Objective 2: Ask pupils to list five new words that may add the suffix *-ion* and use each word in a sentence. They may use their dictionaries to find examples and to mark the accented syllable in each.

Extension Activities

Objective 5: Have pupils pick two of their favorite characters from the story and write a brief descriptive paragraph of each. They should include general traits of the character and some specific situations in which the character demonstrates these traits.

IV. ENRICHMENT

- Pupils may take this opportunity to learn more about various aspects of African history and culture. Divide pupils into groups according to their interests, such as literature, music, art, education, geography, clothing, food, homes, etc. Give each group time to do research and to gather material for a presentation to the class.

- Man's enchantment with the moon is timeless. Early man was fascinated by the moon's unearthly light and its changing shape. Even today, superstitions about the moon continue to haunt men's lives. Mainly because of its changing shape, the moon came to be associated in mythology and folklore with death and rebirth, magic, sorcery, and initiation rites. Pupils may wish to read other myths about the moon or to write their own original myth or folktale about the moon.

- Several of the more advanced pupils may wish to report to the class some interesting facts about the moon and how scientists think it originated. Have pupils use the encyclopedia and periodicals to answer questions such as these:

  Why do we see only one side of the moon?
  Does the moon really change its shape?
  What is the moon made of?
  How does the moon affect the tides?

  Pupils can portray a lunar phenomena, such as an eclipse, by using a flashlight and some rubber balls. Recent photographs of the moon, obtainable from NASA in Washington, D.C., would be an interesting addition to this report.

- Have pupils talk about the impact of science on the world. Ask, "Do you think science can solve most of man's problems and give us a better world tomorrow? Or will science create more problems than it will solve?" Try to stimulate pupils to provide specific examples in support of their opinions.

  Some examples in support of the first question include scientific advances in agriculture, the elimination of many diseases, and the seemingly limitless uses of atomic power for peaceful purposes. To back up affirmative answers to the second question, pupils could cite the atomic and hydrogen bombs, the widening gap between rich nations and poor, and the fact that the world suffers from serious problems of pollution brought on in large part by advances in scientific technology.

Conceptual Background and the Ability of the Learner

Just as reading is limited by the experience of the learner, so is it limited by his conceptual development. A reader cannot read written language that expresses concepts that are far beyond his developed ability to understand. Concepts may be attained through reading, but they must be broadly within the grasp of the reader. Beyond this point, a learner must have help in understanding concepts before he can read. Indeed, teachers would be unneeded if this were not true.

Overdependence on independent study of textbooks in many classrooms is often present because of a confusion between language and the concepts it conveys. Concepts are not only communicated from person to person through language; language is also the symbolic medium individuals use to manipulate their experiences and ideas in order to develop concepts. But language can be manipulated by children without their understanding the concepts involved. A child may state correctly that Michigan is a peninsula and that so is Florida, without grasping the basic significance of peninsularity. He may just be repeating, appropriately, statements he has heard. Similarly, he may read from a text and even supply correct answers to questions at the end of each chapter without in any way understanding the concepts. *Question:* What is Gloopy? *Answer:* Glóópy is a borp.

Some teachers naïvely assume that if a child can translate the written symbols in a text into oral speech, he is capable of dealing with the concepts being presented. If he cannot read a particular word, the teacher considers this a vocabulary problem. But what is labeled a "reading vocabulary problem" may involve problems on four very different levels. Here are four cases to illustrate these levels of vocabulary difficulty:

1. The reader understands a word or phrase—*monkey* or *stationery,* for example—and uses it in his oral speech, but does not recognize its graphic representation.

2. The reader does not know or use the word or phrase in his oral language but can grasp the meaning, particularly in familiar natural language. His previous experience and conceptual development have made this easy addition to his vocabulary possible.

3. The reader does not know or use the word or phrase in his oral language and cannot understand the meaning because it depends on experiences and a level of concept development that he has not attained.

4. The reader can tell the name of the word or phrase, using cues within words, but he does not know, use, or understand what he is reading. Because he does not understand, he is not reading.

Vital contributions to the act of reading, then, are made by the systems of cues and responses to cues that are within or must develop within the reader. To recapitulate, these are

1. Language facility, the internalization of a dialect
2. The physiology of the learner, as it affects perception and expression
3. Learned response, attacks, skills, and learning strategies
4. The experiential background of the reader
5. The reader's conceptual background and ability

From *Language and Thinking in the Elementary School.*

(space)craft

From Old English (OE) *craefte*, power or skill. As a terminal combining form, *-craft* means work, skill, or practice. Compare *aircraft, handicraft*.

Man on the Moon

The suited-up astronauts—Neil A. Armstrong, Edwin E. Aldrin, and Michael Collins—prepare to enter the van that will take them to the launch pad.

The *Apollo 11* spacecraft lifts off at 9:32 A.M., July 16, 1969.

The flight is watched carefully by the Operations Director and his staff at the Goddard Space Flight Center.

FACING PAGE: The Lunar Module is seen behind Edwin Aldrin setting up an experiment on the moon.

Earth can be seen rising above the moon's horizon.

The three astronauts relax in a life raft after their safe splashdown in the Pacific Ocean.

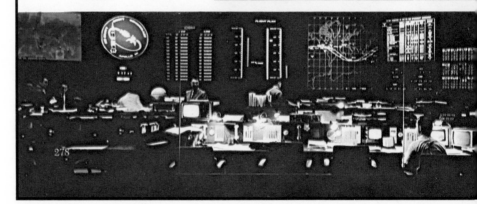

MAN ON THE MOON

THINKING CRITICALLY

Do you think people who are able to land men on the moon would have much use for a myth like the one you just read? (They might read it for enjoyment but not to furnish themselves with an explanation of the origin of the moon.) How does a technologically advanced people go about satisfying their curiosity about space? (Invent, test, research, explore.)

Choose three pupils to read aloud the captions that go with each of the three photographs on this page.

UNDERSTANDING CAUSE AND EFFECT

MAKING COMPARISONS

Why are the astronauts dressed as they are? (The absence of oxygen on the moon requires them to carry oxygen; the suits protect them from possible contamination and enable them to maintain body temperature.) Do the uniforms of the astronauts suggest any other kinds of clothing worn by scientists? (They resemble in some ways the costumes of surgeons working in a hospital room or of men who work in atomic energy plants.)

Choose three pupils to read aloud the captions that go with the photographs on this page.

What is causing the shadows on the moon in the photograph on the top left? (The sun.) Why is the picture of the earth seen as a hemisphere? (Because it is partially blocked by the moon.)

THINKING CRITICALLY

This was a three-stage rocket. Only one part of the vehicle returned with the spacemen to Earth—the command module pictured at the bottom of this page. Looking back at the photograph of the whole rocket on page 278, can you find the command module? (It can be seen near the tip of the rocket.)

DISTINGUISHING A PART FROM THE WHOLE

After seeing these photographs, pupils may want to know such things as exactly how rockets are fired and the nature of the communication between the men in the rocket and those in the Space Center; have pupils suggest questions and choose topics to research.

EXTENDING UNDERSTANDING THROUGH RESEARCH

SKY
of
Sea
High
Deep
As the
A blue
So bright
So new
So old
No other blue
To you
What is the bluest blue?

CLAUDIA LEWIS
Blue

280

Claudia Lewis
For biographical information, see annotation on page 215.

BLUE

NOTING TYPOGRAPHICAL
VARIATION

Introduce the poem by noting that the movement of type on the left-hand page is upward, the movement on the right-hand page is downward. This is a cue that the poem must be read from the bottom of the page on the left, upward to the word *sky*, and downward on the right-hand page. The more able pupils will see this, but others may not. The shape of the poem resembles a rocket's flight.

After the poem has been read and the image of the earth as seen from space described, ask pupils how they have seen the earth. Most of us see it extending outward in a plane.

What is the bluest blue?
  To the astronaut ace
    Afloat
      In space,
        Ringing,
          Swinging,
            Rocket-hurled,
              No other blue
                So new
                  So bright
                    A blue
                      As the
                        Great
                          Blue
                            Ball
                              of the
                              WORLD

281

How far can we see? Where is the horizon and about how far? Have you seen the earth from the top of a mountain? from a skyscraper? from a sand dune by the sea? from a basement window? as a map in a geography book? as a globe? How do we know that the earth is not exactly spherical, but somewhat pear-shaped?

Have pupils locate pictures of the earth from books about the astronauts or from the *National Geographic Magazine*.

"Blue" is taken from *Poems of Earth and Space* by Claudia Lewis. Suggest that pupils may want to read more poems like this one from that book.

RELATING READING TO
EXPERIENCE

Use the sound filmstrip *Finding Patterns in Words*. It presents many examples of word transformation. The main purpose here is to show the principle that affixation in English is derived largely from Old English, Latin, and Greek; and to establish with increasing force the idea that knowledge of morphemes is essential to word mastery.

FINDING PATTERNS IN WORDS

There are many ways of putting words together in English. Sometimes we combine two or more words to make one word. Sometimes we add prefixes and suffixes borrowed from Greek, Latin, or Old English. The exercises below will show you some of the ways of putting words together.

Some Words from Old English

Upward and downward,
All forenoon, all afternoon,
On highways and byways,
Onward and offward,
Underneath and overhead,
Whirled the great wind!

How does each underscored word part give you the idea of time or place or direction? On a sheet of paper, copy each underscored word part on a separate line. Then add a different second part to each word. For example, you could write *upstairs*. Add as many words as you can to each line. Use a dictionary if you need one. All the underlined word parts are from Old English.

282

FINDING PATTERNS IN WORDS

NOTING OLD-ENGLISH WORD PARTS

Have pupils check an encyclopedia and report briefly on when ancient Greek, Latin, and Old English were in use. Indicate that the English alphabet is based on the Greek and Roman alphabets.

Note that the underscored word parts are words used in everyday speech. These are well-established words familiar to most of us, less "ornate" than some we shall study later. Each one may be used separately as a word; each one may be combined with other words.

From Latin

English has borrowed from Latin a number of prefixes that show time, direction, or place. First, study the chart; then read each sentence below and tell how the italicized word makes use of one of the prefixes in the chart.

trans- "across"	super- "over"	pre- "before"	in- "in" or "into"
sub- "under"	post- "after"	ante- "before"	re- "backward" or "again"
per- "through"	ex- "from" or "outward"	circum- "around"	ab- "from" or "away"

1. We sailed on a *transoceanic* liner.
2. John's father is a *supersalesman.*
3. He arrived on a *predawn* flight.
4. *Insert* a coin in the parking meter.
5. We take the *subway* to school.
6. Do you mind if we *postpone* the ball game?
7. Meet me in the *anteroom* after lunch.
8. *Refresh* yourself with lemonade.
9. We watched the bears *perform* in the circus.
10. Maria is an *exchange* student from Mexico.
11. Sir Francis Chichester *circumnavigated* the globe.
12. We may be *absent* on Monday.

Now write twelve sentences, using words with the prefixes in the chart above. Do not use the italicized words in the preceding sentences. Check your dictionary if you need help.

283

Note that the Latin prefixes are followed by hyphens. These indicate that other word parts must be attached. Note that most of these prefixes cannot stand alone as English words. A few, however, may in legal language, often Latinate, act as words: *per, ex, re;* in such cases their meanings generally differ from the prefixal meanings.

Could *overseas* replace *transoceanic* in sentence 1? (Yes.) Does *postpone* mean about the same as *put off?* (Yes.) Does *front hall* mean about the same as *anteroom?* (Yes.) Does *sailed around* mean about the same as *circumnavigated?* (Yes.) Do you think English would be easier if we had only one meaning for each word? How did Latin provide us with a wider range of words? (By adding new forms.)

Have pupils check a collegiate dictionary and introduce additional sample words that begin with the four cited prefixes. Here again, the prefixes do not occur as separate words. Contrast them with the Old English prefixes on page 282.

From Greek

English has also borrowed prefixes which show direction or place from Greek. Among them are the following:

meta-	"along with" or "after"
hyper-	"over," "above," or "beyond"
peri-	"all around"
sym-	"with"

Which word in each of the sentences below uses one of the prefixes defined above?

1. Since I share your sorrow, you have my sympathy.
2. When we measure the four sides of a square, we find its perimeter.
3. The change from a caterpillar to a butterfly is called metamorphosis.
4. If you find fault with everything, you are hypercritical.

Oh, No!

Perhaps the quickest way to say "no" is simply to say "no." But here are some other ways that we use to change a word from a "yes" to a "no" or negative meaning.

284

USING GREEK ROOTS

The word *scope* comes to us from Greek and its root means *to see*. What device does a submarine commander use to see above water? (A periscope.) The word *phone* also comes from Greek and its root means *sound*. With the sounds of all instruments playing together, what kind of orchestra do we name by combining *sym* with *phone*? (Symphony.) *Sonas* is a Latin word that means *sound*. Have you ever heard a sonic boom? (This happens when a plane or missile traveling faster than sound breaks the sound barrier.) What do you think *hypersonic* means? (About five times greater than the speed of sound.)

a-	anti-, ant-	counter-	in-
"no, not"	"against"	"against"	"not"
mis-	**non-**	**ob-**	**un-**
"wrong"	"not"	"against"	"not"

Now write the numbers from 1 to 10 in a column on a sheet of paper. In each of the following sentences, find the word that uses one of the above prefixes. Copy it on your paper after the proper number. Underline the prefix.

1. Marsha is able to come, but Jan is unable.
2. Although Mike is quite capable, Jerry is incapable.
3. If you do not favor going, tell me your objection.
4. *Tall* is the antonym of *short.*
5. After I dictated my plans, he contradicted them.
6. With all those claims and counterclaims, who is right?
7. With winter coming on, Dad filled the car with some antifreeze.
8. Water conducts electricity, but glass is considered a nonconductor.
9. I have no feelings about that; I am apathetic.
10. Judy behaves, whereas Sandy misbehaves.

A good reader increases his vocabulary when he learns how word patterns operate. You have learned how word parts can help you to know direction and place and how word parts can say "no." You will learn to read better if you work to master word meanings.

285

Our book has shown us how prefixes enter English from other languages. Below are listed some prefixes that give us a sense of number. What words or word parts can you add to these prefixes to make whole words?

USING PREFIXES OF NUMBER

bi-	tri-	quart	quint-
(two)	(three)	(four)	(five)
sex-	sept-	pan-	poly-
(six)	(seven)	(all)	(many)

Have pupils check a collegiate dictionary for sample words. Suggest that prefixes help us classify words into particular sets, denoting negatives, numeration, direction, and time.

Look back to the pictures on the Table of Contents page for this unit. Would you have chosen these pictures to illustrate this unit?

USING PICTURE CLUES

UNIT REVIEW

I. SUMMARY ACTIVITIES

After reading the stories, poems, and essays in Unit 3, pupils should have acquired some appreciation of the importance of science and technology to everyday living. They should have begun to realize that developments such as moon landings are dependent upon an accumulation of many scientific discoveries. The historic televised activities on the moon's surface would never have been achieved if changes in the moon were believed to be caused by a sky man's hunger. Today's factories, television, and computers would not exist if electricity were not readily available. Ask pupils to think of any one thing in their lives that is not dependent upon some technological or scientific development of the past. Ask them what they think life would be like without the products of science and technology. Do they think life would be simpler, pleasanter, or harsher and with less leisure time?

To evaluate pupils' understanding of Unit 3 as a whole, develop with them a chart similar to the one below. Write the selection titles and the headings on the board and let the class supply the other material. Relate the technological developments covered in one selection to those in another. For example, a discussion of an evening news telecast may lead to recognition of the relationship between television and space technology. Elicit the fact that advances in space science and rocketry have provided the satellite pictures used to forecast the weather.

Ask pupils to list as many ways as they can in which computers have become part of their everyday lives. Ask them to predict future uses of computers to benefit mankind.

TITLE	AUTHOR	GENRE	RELATIONSHIP TO TECHNOLOGY
"The Television-Chocolate Room"	Roald Dahl	Science fiction	Depicts imagined technological developments of the future
"What Television Is"	Jeanne and Robert Bendick	Essay	Explains modern technology in the field of television
"One for the Univac"	Ethelyn M. Parkinson	Humorous fiction	Relates humorous incident about children trying to imitate a computer
"Computers in Our World"	Alfred Lewis	Essay	Explains contributions of computers to the space program and to everyday life
"Robert H. Goddard: Father of the Space Age"	Clyde B. Moore	Biography	Describes the research involved in developments of space rocketry
"By the Light of the Moon"	Alfred Slote	Folk tale	Shows that long before science helped to explain things, men created stories to explain the natural occurrences which they observed

II. REVIEW EXERCISES

To review the major skills developed in Unit 3, the following three sets of exercises may be used: A. Reading and Language, B. Comprehension and Literary Skills, and C. Study Skills. These exercises may be duplicated and distributed to pupils as needed.

A. Reading and Language

1. Look at the following words. Draw a line between syllables of those words that have more than one syllable, as you would pronounce them.

1. teach/er   6. south/ern
2. sys/tem   7. flick/er

3. dazz/ling   8. crease
4. cre/ate   9. chil/dren
5. splash/ing   10. catch/ing

2. Look at the words in the following list and read the sentences that follow them. In the blank in each sentence, write the correct word from the list. Use each word only once.

circumnavigate   predetermine   subnormal
excavate   transoceanic   transmit
precede   refit

1. To sail around the world would be to   circumnavigate   the world.

2. To send a message across a distance would be to
   transmit   the message.

3. If the speech comes before the luncheon, the
   speech is said to   precede   the meal.

4. To prepare to use a ship again is to
   refit   the ship.

5. To decide what to do beforehand is to   predetermine   what you will do.

6. To dig a hole in the ground is to   excavate   .

7. A ship that goes across the ocean is called a
   transoceanic   liner.

8. To have a temperature below 98.6 degrees is to
   have a   subnormal   temperature.

3. Look at the following words. In the blank before each word, write *B* if the word is formed from a base word and an affix, and *R* if the word is formed from a Latin root and an affix. Underline the base word or the root in each word.

B 1. uneasy   R 6. recline

R 2. permit   B 7. washer

R 3. complete   B 8. redo

B 4. disagree   R 9. distaste

B 5. happily   R 10. progress

4. The words in the list below contain an Old English prefix of direction or time. Select the correct word from the list and write it in the blank to complete the sentences that follow.

afterthought   highbrow   overboard
bypass   offhand   underhanded
downstairs   onset   upturn
forethought

1. Without a watch, I can only tell you the time
   offhand   .

2. A little   forethought   will help you prepare your
   homework.

3. To miss the midtown traffic, we took the un-
   paved   bypass   .

4. Albert Einstein Smedley was considered a
   highbrow   .

5. After so much bad luck, we can only hope for
   an   upturn   .

6. As an   afterthought   , he included Rupert on the
   team.

7. They put sandbags along the levees before the
   onset   of the hurricane.

8. His   underhanded   trick will not soon be for-
   given.

9. They threw the shark repellent   overboard   .

10. The baby took his first steps when he fell
    downstairs   .

5. In the blank after each word, write the base word. Then select a word from the list to complete each sentence below and write it in the blank.

1. decoration   decorate

2. conference   confer

3. observance   observe

4. exhibition   exhibit

5. completion   complete

6. The   exhibition   had many interesting displays.

7. Mary's teacher called her mother in for a
   conference.

8. The blue   decoration   is beautiful.

9. In   observance   of the holiday, flags were flown.

10. Upon   completion   of the work, a party was held.

6. Draw a line under the prepositional phrase markers in the following sentences. Draw a second line under the entire phrase.

1. The animals got their food from Mbui and Etuk.

2. Lindbergh helped Goddard get the money for

   his experiments.

3. Computers have been called by many names.

4. What TV program do you watch at six o'clock?   **T•489**

5. In our family we take turns selecting programs.

6. Are you going to the circus?

7. The treasure was buried under a big oak tree.

8. All members of our baseball team have new uniforms.

9. Rupert's mother was standing on the back porch with the other ladies.

10. Mike ran across the room to the television camera.

7. In the following sentences, underline each pronoun. In the blank after the sentence, write the noun the pronoun is substituted for, along with the noun marker if there is one.

1. "The chocolate is gone!" shouted Grandpa Joe as he watched it disappear.   Grandpa Joe,
the chocolate

2. The animals refused to give Mbui food when he asked for it.   Mbui, food

3. The townspeople helped the Goddards get settled when they arrived in New Mexico.
the Goddards

4. The apes ate the bananas, and then they told the wild pigs where to get them.   The apes, the
bananas

5. Albert was inside the Univac while Mrs. Smedley was looking for him.   Albert

8. Look at the list of pronouns and the sentences below. Replace the underlined words in each sentence with one of the pronouns from the list and rewrite the sentence in the space provided.

I	they	it	them	their
we	he	him	us	my
she	me	her	his	our

1. Dick, John, and I ate most of the candy that had been sent to Dick, John, and me.
We ate most of the candy that had been sent to us.

2. Mr. Teavee took Mike's holster away.
He took his holster away.

3. Annabelle's mother wanted Annabelle to do the dishes.
Her mother wanted her to do the dishes.

4. Rupert, Clayte, and Dood used lights in the Univac.
They used them in the Univac.

5. Mr. and Mrs. Smedley's plan was to win fame for Albert.
Their plan was to win fame for him.

9. In each row of words below, cross out the one word that does not fit in the same category as the other words.

1. battery	motor	generator	olives
2. easel	horn	brushes	paint
3. square	triangle	shingle	rectangle
4. collar	necktie	necklace	bracelet
5. bread	apples	pears	peaches

B. Comprehension and Literary Skills

1. In each sentence below, underline the word that imitates a sound.
1. We talked while the machinery hummed in the background.
2. Mary jumped in surprise when the logs in the fireplace began to crackle.
3. The clock was ticking away the hours as the noisy party continued.
4. Hurriedly, Billy swished the dishrag across the dishes.
5. The rustling of the leaves and the cries of the birds were signs that a storm was coming.

2. Look at the following sentences. Write F in the blank if the statement is one of fact; write O if the statement is one of opinion.

O 1. Computers will put too many people out of jobs.
F 2. The main job of a computer is to count or to figure.
F 3. Computers are quite different from mechanical monsters.
O 4. Computers use too much electricity.
F 5. The waves of television signals are not as long as regular radio waves.
O 6. Channel 2 has the best programs on Friday nights.

F   7. Some people use transistor radios.

O   8. Radio newcasts are better than television newcasts.

F   9. A car radio enables one to listen while driving.

F 10. Radio was invented before television.

3. Read the following paragraphs carefully. Under-line the sentence that states the main idea in each paragraph.

   1. Years ago people lived by the changing phases

      of the moon. They kept holidays and calendars

      by the moon. They planted seeds in the spring's new moon and harvested in the autumn's full moon. Fishermen all over the world told tomor-row's weather by the moon.

   2. Computers do more than compute. One of their

      talents is comparing one number with another. They can compare one name with an entirely different one, one meter reading with an earlier record. Because they can compare, they can also select and sort and obey instructions.

   3. But television is more than just a picture sent by radio waves and seen across space. Television is

      the greatest way ever invented for sending infor-

      mation across space. More people than ever

      before can now both see and hear the sights, sounds, and ideas of the world they live in.

4. Listed after each title below are three settings where some of the action of the selection could have taken place. In the blank before each title, write the letter of the setting that does not occur in the selections.

   b 1. "The Television-Chocolate Room"
          a. a TV screen b. a TV signal-relay station c. a factory elevator.

   c 2. "One for the Univac"
          a. The Pipers' backyard b. Legion Hall c. a piano-box tree house

   a 3. "Robert H. Goddard: Father of the Space Age"
          a. Cape Kennedy, Florida b. Roswell, New Mexico c. Eden Valley

   b 4. "By the Light of the Moon"
          a. a cocoyam farm b. the moon's surface c. an East African riverbank

   c 5. "Man on the Moon"
          a. Apollo 11 launch pad b. the moon's surface c. Atlantic Ocean

C. Study Skills

1. Look at the following questions. Decide where you would look to find the answer to each. In the blank before each question, write E if you would look in an encyclopedia, D if in a dictionary, and A if in an atlas.

   A   1. Does the border of India touch the border of China?

   D   2. Can pain be used both as a noun and as a verb?

   D   3. What is the plural of hippopotamus?

   E   4. Who founded the city of Chicago?

   A   5. Is Detroit closer to Chicago than Indianapolis is?

   D   6. Does combine have more than one pronun-ciation?

   E   7. How many plays did Shakespeare write?

   E   8. Can whales breathe underwater?

   A   9. Is Boston closer to Cleveland or to Miami?

   D 10. What is the plural of sheep?

III.   CREATIVE ACTIVITIES

A. In a brief paragraph or two, answer the following questions.

   1. How might the folktale in "By the Light of the Moon," have ended if the animals had given Mbui food?

   2. How might "One for the Univac" have ended if Mrs. Smedley had been angry because Albert was in the Univac?

   3. What might have happened if only parts of Mike Teavee had appeared on the television screen?

   4. How do you feel about Mike Teavee's attitude toward television? Would you have done what he did?

   5. Compare the resourcefulness of Mike Teavee in "The Television-Chocolate Room" with that of Rupert Piper in "One for the Univac."

B. Put yourself in one of the following situations and write a letter of application that you think will get you what you want.

   1. You have heard about Willy Wonka's offer to allow five children to tour his chocolate factory. You wish to be one of the five lucky ones. Write him a letter explaining why you want to be chosen.

2. NASA is offering free education through college to young scientists in exchange for five years' work on the space program. You have always dreamed of being part of the space program. Write NASA a letter explaining why you feel you deserve to be chosen.

3. You think you have created a new and daring television program to provide education and entertainment for all ages. You want a chance to present your show to an audience. Write a letter to the local station manager outlining your show and explaining why it should be aired.

TEACHER'S NOTES

TEACHER'S NOTES

TEACHER'S NOTES

TEACHER'S NOTES